FORTNIGHT

IN THE

PHILIPPINES

Meira bat Erachaim

ISBN: 1497499984
ISBN-13: 978-1497499980

To the people of the Philippines.

CONTENTS

ACKNOWLEDGEMENTS

This is a personal account of specific disaster response operations carried out by one search and rescue team in the aftermath of Typhoon Haiyan in November 2013. It is not a general report on Israel Defense Forces in the Philippines and is not intended to represent all IDF operations or those conducted by other states.

This work is neither authorised nor endorsed by the Israel Defense Forces. The opinions expressed herein are those of the author and do not necessarily reflect the opinions of the IDF, the government of Israel, or any of its officers or agencies.

No classified or restricted information is contained herein and no attempt has been made to circumvent the laws of the State of Israel or the IDF's ru'ah tzahal.

Statistical data and figures are from a variety of sources. Information relating to specific country delegations is from the respective agencies of those countries.

Israeli figures are from the IDF Operations Directorate.

American figures are from the US Department of Defense.

Canadian figures are from the Canadian Armed Forces.

Casualty figures are from the National Disaster Risk Reduction and Management Council, an agency of the Philippines Department of National Defense.

Storm figures are from the Joint Typhoon Warning Center, an agency of the United States Navy and Air Force.

Additional statistics are from the United Nations Office for the Coordination of Humanitarian Affairs.

Satellite images courtesy of NASA Goddard MODIS Rapid Response Team.

Israel Aerospace Industries LTD is an aircraft defence corporation owned by the state of Israel.

Sikorsky Aircraft is an aviation subsidiary of United Technologies Corporation.

This book would not have been possible without the efforts of Colonel Ramtin Sabti, Dr David Dagan, Lieutenant Colonel Dr Ofer Merin, Gail Roska, Bibi Delos Reyes, and the countless volunteers, Filipino and foreign, who worked in adverse conditions to assist the people of the Philippines however possible.

INTRODUCTION

Typhoon Haiyan slammed into the Philippines at 315 kilometres per hour on Friday 8 November 2013. It had already hit Palau and parts of Micronesia at lower speeds, causing far less damage. Haiyan was at its peak when it hit the Philippines.

Wind speed numbers vary depending on the source. Some agencies measure ten minute sustained winds and others measure one minute sustained winds. The experts are debating whether Haiyan is the fourth largest or the largest typhoon ever recorded. But they all agree that it was the largest storm to ever hit land when it impacted the Philippines.

Some have said that there should be a new classification system and that Haiyan should be a Category 6 typhoon. The current scale changes every 30 to 40 kilometres per hour. A Category 1 typhoon has wind speeds of 119 to

153 kilometres per hour. Category 2 is 154 to 177, Category 3 is 178 to 208, Category 4 is 209 to 251, Category 5 is anything above 252 kilometres per hour. But as storms get stronger and winds over 300 kilometres per hour become more common they might want to alter the categories. Following the current pattern, Haiyan could easily be a Category 6 or 7, if such a thing existed.

There were plenty of warnings that Typhoon Haiyan was going to hit the Philippines, as there always are. Typhoons give you several days to prepare. The Philippines is the type of country that is generally always on alert during typhoon season, typically between July to October. Storms in the last few years have been coming sooner and dying out later, so a large typhoon in November was not especially surprising.

Any number of small typhoons and tropical storms hit the Philippines every year. The people who live there are as accustomed to typhoons as the people in Turkey are to earthquakes and the people of Malibu to watching their houses fall off of cliffs.

Everybody was ready for Typhoon Haiyan. Except that they were not. It was always predicted to be large but there is the very real possibility that many people assumed it would be just another typhoon. When you live somewhere that gets hit by a dozen typhoons every year you quickly lose interest.

Everybody knew that Haiyan would be large but my impression is that nobody appreciated how much damage it would cause. I think this is foolish. Apathy toward storms only makes sense if none of them are predicted to be enormous super typhoons. Unlike an earthquake that can suddenly kill thousands of people in a few minutes, typhoons always give plenty of advance warning. Basic preparedness could have saved a few thousand lives in this instance.

People in Palau were ordered to evacuate. Most refused. No matter where you are in the world you can always find people who would rather die than leave their homes for a day or two. We humans are very territorial creatures.

Almost one million people in the Philippines were evacuated into temporary shelters and designated evacuation centres. But this would prove inadequate as well over 10 million people would be affected by Typhoon Haiyan and 530 704 were rendered homeless on impact. A week after the typhoon there would be 1 871 321 homeless. That number would quickly escalate to 4.4 million. An estimated 300 000 people made their way to evacuation centres the day after the storm.

Typhoon Haiyan was considerably smaller when it hit Palau. As a category 2 storm it brought far less wind and rain. And in Palau there were none of the tsunami like waves that destroyed Tacloban and much of eastern Leyte. As Palau is a very small island, Haiyan passed over it fairly quickly. There were no deaths reported in Palau and less than 100 people were left homeless. This might have given the people of the Philippines the wrong impression.

I appreciate that I have the luxury of living in a country that is immune to most natural disasters. Tropical cyclones are impossible anywhere near my house. Tsunamis are possible but highly unlikely. We have a relatively comprehensive drainage system that makes flooding difficult and rarely results in fatalities. We are prone to earthquakes but there has not been any catastrophic destruction since 1837. The most threatening natural disasters to face my country are wildfires. And they are largely preventable.

I have lived in other places that are magnets for natural disasters, however. I briefly lived in China where earthquakes are a regular occurrence. The Chinese government, flawed as it may be in many respects, thinks ahead when it comes to building construction codes. Anything greater than two floors has to be steel reinforced concrete with fire retardant materials. When a building collapses in an earthquake, as many schools did in the 2008 Wenchuan earthquake, it is more often than not because corners were cut and bribes were accepted to look the other way. But the laws, when enforced, are more than adequate.

I went to university in California, which is home to earthquakes, brush fires, landslides, floods. Earthquakes are impossible to predict but easy to prepare for, even under California's relatively lenient construction codes. Most of the brush fires in California are the result of arson or neglect. It is the landslides that sail through the changing ocean tides and catch people unprepared.

Typhoons should be easier since they let you know days in advance that they are coming. I am not suggesting that everybody should panic at the first storm warning but many lives could be saved if people simply pay attention and evacuate the areas that everybody knows will be hit the hardest. Our inherent disinterest in evacuating is probably the greater threat.

The good news is that people are always willing to help each other after a natural disaster. We may show apathy before disasters and ignore ways to prevent them but we always provide whatever assistance we can after the fact.

Countries all over the world gave all manner of humanitarian aid to the Philippines in the wake of Typhoon Haiyan. Supplies were shipped in by the planeload every day for weeks. Australia, Canada, China, Israel, Japan, the United Kingdom and United States sent a considerable number of relief personnel. Nine other countries sent smaller teams. Over 60 different countries sent money and supplies. During the search and rescue stage there were over 3000 foreigners in the Philippines assisting with relief efforts.

This is the story of one of those search and rescue teams.

Timeline of Events

Friday 8 November 2013.

• Typhoon Haiyan impacts, halting all water, electricity, communication, transportation.

• Almost one million people evacuated to improvised shelters.

Saturday 9 November. Moderate rain, scattered showers.

• Typhoon Haiyan heads to China and Vietnam.

• Sporadic looting begins in Visayas region.

• Conflicting reports on the number of dead and missing.

• An additional 300 000 arrive at evacuation centres.

Sunday 10 November. Light rain, partly cloudy.

• IsraAid and Médecins Sans Frontières teams arrive in Tacloban.

• An estimated 10 million people have been affected by the storm.

• 229 confirmed dead, 45 injured, 28 missing.

Monday 11 November. Cloudy, scattered showers.

• Philippines government declares state of national calamity.

• Telecommunications partially established.

• IDF Home Front Command unit arrive in Cebu.

Tuesday 12 November. Heavy rain.

• 4.8 magnitude earthquake reported in the Visayas.

• Philippines government begins fixing prices.

• 1798 confirmed dead, 2582 injured, 82 missing.

Wednesday 13 November. Moderate to heavy rain throughout the day.

• 530 704 people are homeless.

• 2344 confirmed dead, 3804 injured, 109 missing.

Thursday 14 November. Scattered showers.

• Israeli delegation arrive in Cebu, begin construction of field hospital in Bogo.

• American aircraft carrier USS *George Washington* arrives in Eastern Visayas.

• Canadian personnel and equipment arrive in Iloilo.

• 2537 confirmed dead, 4053 injured, 177 missing.

Friday 15 November. Partly cloudy.

• Habitat for Humanity distributes 500 emergency shelter kits.

• Israeli field hospital fully functional, treats 140 patients, delivers first typhoon baby.

• 375 795 people throughout Philippines assisted through food distribution.

• 1 871 321 are homeless.

Saturday 16 November. Moderate rain.

• Philippines government begins airdrops of relief supplies to remote areas.

• 370 people, including 150 children, treated at field hospital.

• 5 million children affected by storm. 3 million homeless, with 371 000 living in 1086 evacuation centres.

• Local agencies begin digging mass graves.

• 3631 confirmed dead, 12501 injured, 1186 missing.

Sunday 17 November. Moderate rain.

• Field hospital treats 582 patients, including 244 children, delivers 3 babies in 1 hour.

• Infrastructure teams install water cistern on islands without access.

• Water restored to 80% of Tacloban.

• 3976 confirmed dead, 15718 injured, 1590 missing.

Monday 18 November. Heavy rain.

• Australian delegation build field hospital in Tacloban.

• Israeli field hospital treats 952 patients.

• School year begins. IDF teams repair school, teach a few classes.

• 837 900 food packages delivered.

• 4011 confirmed dead, 18175 injured, 1602 missing.

Tuesday 19 November. Moderate rain.

• 85% of phone networks established in Visayas.

• Field hospital treats 1000th patient, relief teams distribute over 200 meals to nearby villages.

• International media cancels coverage.

• 4.4 million people are homeless.

Wednesday 20 November. Heavy rain, electrical storms.

• 1451 patients treated at field hospital, including 463 children.

• 4623 confirmed dead, 18557 injured, 1602 missing.

Thursday 21 November. Moderate to heavy rain, scattered storms.

• China sends hospital ship, 和平方舟 (*Peace Ark*), with 100 medical personnel to southern Visayas.

• 2 more schools on Cebu Island rebuilt.

• 1 out of every 3 patients is a child.

Friday 22 November. Moderate rain, electrical storms.

• Full Japanese delegation arrive in Eastern Visayas.

• Israeli field hospital treats 2000th patient.

• 5209 confirmed dead, 23404 injured, 1611 missing.

Saturday 23 November. Moderate to heavy rain.

• Additional medical supplies and equipment arrive in Cebu.

• 5235 confirmed dead, 24681 injured, 1673 missing.

Sunday 24 November. Moderate rain, scattered thunderstorms.

• New water filtration system built in northern Cebu.

• 5387 confirmed dead, 25074 injured, 1708 missing.

Monday 25 November. Light to moderate rain.

• British aircraft carrier HMS *Illustrious* arrives in Visayas.

• More repaired schools reopen.

• 5469 confirmed dead, 25916 injured, 1747 missing.

Tuesday 26 November. Heavy rain, storms throughout the Visayas.

• 5560 confirmed dead, 26194 injured, 1726 missing.

Wednesday 27 November. Scattered showers.

• IDF delegation depart the Philippines, leave equipment and supplies to local hospital and Austrian delegation.

ONE

Typhoon Haiyan hit Eastern Samar on the Pacific Ocean side of the Visayas just before dawn on Friday 8 November, bringing with it instant floods and 5 metre coastal waves. It then hit Leyte Island with 6 metre waves and tore apart 80 percent of the province's houses and infrastructure before moving west.

Cebu Island was still recovering from a 7.2 magnitude earthquake on Bohol Island that killed 222 people and injured 976 on 15 October during the Eid al Adha festival. Houses were still being repaired and more than a few were in the early construction phase. Approximately 40000 people were still living in temporary shelters on Bohol Island. The hospitals were more active than usual. Some were heavily damaged in the earthquake, and treatment was provided in tents and temporary structures. Electricity and water supplies had only recently been restored. Emergency supplies had yet to be repleted. This was arguably the worst time for another natural disaster to hit the area.

Haiyan passed directly over the northern half of Cebu Island. Bohol Island was relatively unscathed but Cebu suffered catastrophic damage.

After tearing through Panay Island, which was also recovering from the earthquake, the typhoon headed west and decimated Busuanga Island whilst causing minor damage to the less populated Palawan area.

It finally made its way out into the South China Sea where it weakened before crashing into Vietnam.

Typhoon Haiyan was large enough to feel like a typhoon, tsunami, and unending tornadoes all rolled into one storm.

Initial reports the day after the storm quickly rose from 3 deaths in Eastern Samar to 200 in Leyte. By the afternoon of Saturday 9 November the local government reported 1000 dead in Tacloban alone. The Red Cross reported 1200 dead.

I was told on 7 November that I would probably be sent to the Philippines. Everybody knew that Haiyan would be a very large super typhoon by then and we assumed that the damage would be extensive. No government agency in the Philippines had asked officially or unofficially for our assistance but we were preparing to give it anyway.

I cannot speak to how far in advance other

countries alert their emergency personnel but in Israel we like to be ready for whatever horrible thing is coming next. I would like to think that the Red Cross was ready to go before the typhoon hit but I have no direct knowledge of their procedures.

Whenever there is any disaster anywhere in the world the United States generally gets all the publicity for sending in whatever assistance is needed. But they are far from the only country that assists in humanitarian efforts. Over 100 different countries sent various forms of humanitarian aid to Haiti after their big earthquake in 2010.

France, once Haiti's overlords, sent military and medical personnel and equipment. Italy sent an aircraft carrier with medical personnel and supplies. China donated millions of dollars, sent in medical personnel, and increased their UN mandated police force. Indonesia and Iran sent medical teams, food, medical supplies. Qatar and Turkey sent in medical personnel, search and rescue teams, equipment and supplies.

South Korea donated more money than almost anybody and sent a search and rescue team. Saudi Arabia donated the most money; 50 million US dollars according to the UN. The United States pledged more money but never actually delivered it.

Israel set up a field hospital and several clinics, sent in medical personnel, search and rescue teams, forensic investigators and police forces. The United States sent several warships, military and medical personnel and equipment but ended medical evacuations prematurely when congressional funding stopped. Another clear example of bureaucracy inaction.

Canada built an airport, sent medical and military personnel, built a field hospital, created a new infrastructure for drinking water. Canada probably did more for Haiti than anybody else but, as usual, was given less credit than the United States. Canadians are used to that.

To be fair, the United States often sends more money, equipment, personnel than any other country. They generally already have a presence wherever disasters strike. It takes little effort for them to send military personnel since they likely have people stationed nearby. The American aircraft carrier sent to the Philippines was stationed just up the block in Hong Kong at the time of the typhoon. The rest of us have to travel around the world to get to the people that need our help.

The United States is also bound by treaties and other agreements to assist many countries where most of us can choose whether we want to help or not. Palau is completely dependent on the United States in a military situation or natural disaster. Should anything happen in Palau the United States is required by law to assist. Such a relationship works to both nations' advantage.

Most countries are small enough that the rest of the world will never depend on us.

I am a junior grade field command officer, NATO OF-3, casualty extraction and medical evacuation pilot, Palmachim 30th Airbase, Helicopter Air Group, Israeli Air Force. I had about 3000 hours PIC in the IAI modified Sikorsky UH-60 as of October 2013. Most of my experience is in hazardous terrain and air-sea rescue with emphasis on combat casualty extraction.

In the wake of a natural disaster it is better to have medical evacuation teams with a greater emphasis on urban search and rescue. Several teams with more than ample experience were sent to the Philippines but a series of minor earthquakes in Israel at the end of October and beginning of November forced the IDF Home Front Command to prepare for a larger earthquake sometime in the near future. It was decided that some of the more experienced teams in urban search and rescue should stay behind in the event that they were needed at home. I would have never gone to the Philippines otherwise.

My team had participated in more than a few search and rescue operations before Typhoon Haiyan but had little experience with multihazard urban search and rescue. The difference is in what you find on the ground and how you proceed.

Hazardous terrain search and rescue involves sending air and land crews into geographically isolated areas or places that are difficult to access, such as mountain ranges, dense forests, deserts. Air-sea rescue is a simple task of locating and extracting survivors in the middle of a vast body of water.

I have been told by movies that it is far easier to spot a person in the middle of the ocean than it is to rescue somebody from the side of a mountain but my experience has been the exact opposite. People on the ground can perform a variety of actions that will make themselves more visible. People in the water are usually too busy trying to stay afloat. And signal fires in a life raft are just a bad idea.

Multihazard urban search and rescue involves locating and extracting survivors from damaged and collapsed urban structures. This is mostly a ground action as spotting a person inside a building from the average helicopter is difficult at best. Those involved need to have extensive knowledge of structural integrity as well as the ability to identify and neutralise the building's electric and gas systems. Hence the multihazard.

This is not to say that the people of the Philippines were somehow short changed by the presence of my team. Our training and experience proved useful in the mountains, seas and thousands of coastline kilometres of the Visayas. My team never went to Haiti but followed the relief efforts just like everybody else and saw it as a good blueprint on which to base any future Philippine operations. Several of our delegation's command officers were involved in constructing the field hospital in Haiti.

We began our preparations before

Typhoon Haiyan even hit the Philippines. My team studied topographic maps and bathymetric charts of the projected impact zone. There was no way to know how much damage the typhoon would cause but we could at least get to know the terrain in which we would likely be working.

Medical officers considered the best ways to set up a field hospital on one of the islands before there was a single casualty. The infrastructure teams thought about roads and water supplies. It simply seemed like the right thing to do.

If it turned out to be as much of a disaster as everybody expected then it was only prudent to be ready to help out as soon as possible. Had the storm changed course and made our assistance unnecessary then our preparations could be considered further training. A little extra training never hurt.

The only problem with being prepared is that others do not always plan ahead as well. No rescue operations or humanitarian aid can be sent into any sovereign country until the leaders of that country request assistance. Nobody, not even the United States, will land any military aircraft onto foreign soil without a formal request. Drones in Pakistan being the exception to the rule. You cannot even send them food and water until they ask for it.

An unfortunate trait in humans is our hubris. We elect or allow leaders who think they can take on any challenge and who, more often than not, refuse to ask for help when it is obviously needed. Our arrogance can be seen in countless disaster situations where the people in charge wait days or even weeks before accepting outside assistance. Some countries refuse aid even when it could save lives.

A recent example is Hurricane Katrina in 2005. Much of the world offered to help but American leaders felt that they were above such need. They refused donations of money from countries they do not like and even from more than a few of their allies. They accepted humanitarian aid from Israel and India but refused to allow IDF search and rescue teams full access. Supplies and equipment were accepted from their European friends but relief personnel were rejected. The resulting chaos and turmoil in New Orleans was an unnecessary embarrassment to that country's leaders and the final death toll could have been much lower.

That level of xenophobia was nothing compared to Myanmar. Cyclone Nargis in 2008 was one of the world's deadliest cyclones, killing at least 100 000 people. There were no benefit concerts in New York. The Myanmar regime accepted money but blocked most humanitarian aid and refused visas for international organisations. Aid workers with extensive disaster relief experience in a variety of climates and topographies were denied entry. Most of the relief supplies that were allowed into the country were never delivered to those in need, according to the UN.

Haiti, in contrast, was quick to ask anybody and everybody for help immediately after their earthquake. Much of the world was quick to respond.

The Philippines initially refused offers of assistance. President Benigno Aquino praised his military leaders whilst insisting that local governments could not do anything to help because they were victims of the typhoon themselves. He told CNN that international aid would be unnecessary.

The government quickly changed their minds when officials started to fully appreciate the level of damage. They were more than grateful for whatever assistance they could get after a local politician overestimated that at least 10000 people were killed in Leyte.

I cannot say when the Philippine government asked others for help but they formally accepted Israel's offer to send medical and rescue personnel on Sunday 10 November. A Home Front Command advance team under the direction of Major General Eyal Eizenberg was sent to the Philippines on Sunday night and immediately set up a base of operations on Cebu Island when they arrived on Monday afternoon.

The advance team comprised of six medical officers and search and rescue specialists whose main purpose was to assess the medical situation, conduct an infrastructure evaluation, determine what additional personnel should be brought in. It took them very little time to decide that medical treatment and search and rescue should be the highest priority. By Monday night General Eizenberg had ordered the formation of Operation Islands of Hope. Say what you will about Israelis but we love to give everything a catchy name.

Nongovernmental organisations such as IsraAid and Médecins Sans Frontières began sending teams over the weekend. They can always respond faster than any military operation. Partly because they do not have to wait for authorisation from different government agencies and mostly because few nations worry about an NGO invasion. Foreign armies of warships and military helicopters tend to make people nervous.

On Tuesday 12 November my team were briefed on our mission in the Philippines. We were told that the Home Front Command advance team had chosen a base of operations north of Cebu City to a more heavily damaged and secluded area. We were all relatively familiar with Cebu Island by then from studying all of the collected intelligence.

It was announced during our briefing that there was a 4.8 magnitude earthquake in the Visayas. It was too small to make any difference but its timing was unwelcome. The 7.2 magnitude Bohol earthquake from October was still on everybody's minds when the typhoon hit. Additional earthquakes or large aftershocks would make life more difficult for everybody. The psychological impact of another disaster at this time on the people of the Philippines could not be dismissed.

Typhoons are better than earthquakes in many ways. They do their damage and go away, leaving everybody free to pick up the pieces. It is highly unlikely that another typhoon will hit as people are cleaning up the first typhoon. Earthquakes almost always come in clusters, hampering rescue and recovery operations. It is very likely that there will be another earthquake whilst people are cleaning up the first one.

If the 4.8 earthquake was only an aftershock of October's 7.2 then there was little to worry about. But if it was a completely new event then more aftershocks or even greater earthquakes could be expected.

Tuesday's earthquake was small but it forced us to think about contingency scenarios. A large earthquake in Manila or Cebu at this time would have absolutely crippled the country.

During our briefing we were told that the looting that began on Saturday was mostly under control. The Philippine government imposed a night curfew and declared a "state of national calamity". This designation allowed local governments to utilise any disaster funds they had; often a significant percentage of their annual budget. It also gave the military the authority to restore order about as well as could be expected.

Many of the local police departments were personally affected by the typhoon and could not be reasonably expected to prevent the looting and other crimes largely unnoticed under such circumstances. All of the police officers in one small Western Visayas village were missing or dead. Nationwide there were 1798 confirmed dead, 2582 injured, 82 missing.

The Israeli base would of course have security and none of us doubted that the field hospital would be well protected. If Israelis know two things one of them is the importance of security.

The other is where to find the best humus. Ask a million Israelis and you will get a million different answers. Obviously it is at that shop around the corner from Abouelafia and Sons in Jaffa. It is a tourist area but there is some great food if you know where to look.

In this case, security was doubtless more important than humus. The last thing anybody needs during emergency surgery is to have some deranged fanatic burst in and start shooting up the place.

We were not worried about it. The field hospital in Haiti had a perimeter fence and guard towers. Extra security precautions were taken because the hospital was set up on the southern end of the island where crime was an issue long before the earthquake and where some of the extremist groups would have loved to put the murder of a Jewish doctor or two on their CVs.

The American delegation in Haiti considered sending an entire aircraft carrier strike group to the other side of the peninsula until somebody decided that it would be more efficient to let the Israeli delegation go to an area where, quite frankly, nobody else wanted to go.

But the Philippines is not Haiti. Crime and political turmoil in the Philippines cannot compare with Haiti on a good day. The level of government corruption is debatable but nobody worried about kidnappings and political executions in the Philippines. The looting that started on Saturday was largely seen as desperate acts of survival rather than any breakdown of society or planned anarchy.

Search and rescue teams such as mine would be away from the protection of a secured field hospital every time we went out to locate survivors or relocate patients but we did not think for a second that looters were going to endanger our mission. Most of them were looking for food and water to feed their families. I doubt any of them set out to pinch a helicopter and a few defibrillators.

We learnt after our Tuesday briefing that the Philippine government began fixing prices in an effort to limit profiteering, which would only result in more looting.

TWO

On Wednesday morning 234 people and 100 tonnes of medical supplies and humanitarian aid were loaded onto two El Al 747s and flew 9000 kilometres from Tel Aviv to Cebu Island in the Central Visayas region of the Philippines. Larger equipment and vehicles had already been transported and were waiting for us when we arrived.

The mood on the flight was enthusiastic. There was not a single person on either of those airliners that did not want to be there. Say what you will about humans, and I am just as guilty of thinking the worst about people as anybody else, but we have a habit of dropping everything and helping out our fellow man in times of crisis. Every single person on that flight to the Philippines volunteered to leave their homes and families to help total strangers who were suffering. If that is not compassion then I cannot say what is.

Reports from the Philippines were that 530 704 people were homeless. 2344 people were confirmed dead, 3804 were injured, and 109 were missing.

We all knew that we would have to get to work as soon as we landed and that sleeping on the flight was probably a good idea. But sleep was the last thing on anybody's mind. We were all eager to hit the ground running. For much of the flight we segregated ourselves into our teams and discussed our mission objectives and how best to approach the task ahead of us.

Eventually some people had a nap. It was a long flight and it took its toll as long flights are wont to do. I slept for about four hours of the 13 hour flight to Cebu.

The city of Tacloban on Leyte Island was thought to be the more devastated area of the country at the time but the airport in Tacloban was partially damaged by Typhoon Haiyan and only open to smaller aircraft. The Mactan-Cebu International Airport was fully operational and quickly became the staging ground for most of the international relief effort.

From Cebu City the Americans, Japanese, Australians, and most of the other delegations went east to Leyte Island and Samar Island. The Chinese delegation went to Leyte and farther south to Bohol Island. The Canadians went west to Panay Island. The British went even farther west to Mimaropa and islands north of Panay. The Israeli delegation went to the northern end of Cebu Island.

It was a unique experience to alight from that aeroplane at the Cebu airport. I have lived close to the Arctic Circle, below the Tropic of Capricorn, and a few places in between. I do not remember ever stepping off an aircraft and feeling such a strong wave of humidity hit every inch of my body. Typhoon Haiyan was long gone but the feeling of a tropical storm still loitered in the air.

For a fleeting moment I almost knew how The Beatles felt when they landed at JFK Airport in 1964. Crowds of Filipinos cheered as we disembarked the aircraft. They were not applauding us personally. They were happy to see every flight that landed that day. I would doubt that any of them were waiting for us to sing a song but it was the first time in my life, and likely last, that I was met at an airport by so many people so grateful to see me.

Ed Sullivan has yet to call.

We could immediately see countless palettes full of supplies from our own 747s and probably dozens of others from as many different countries. Philippine military personnel were loading boxes into cargo trucks faster than we could get down the ramp. We could see a Singapore Air Force C-130 with that distinctive black magpie, or whatever bird that is, on the tail waiting either to take off or land.

You can ordinarily tell whether an aircraft is coming or going based on its orientation but there was a fair amount of organised chaos at the airfield that day. I did not envy the air traffic controllers their jobs. They were victims of the storm themselves yet that control tower remained operational 24 hours a day for at least the next two weeks.

Most of the Israeli medical personnel and infrastructure teams loaded several buses and drove north from Cebu to Bogo City. My team and a few others collected our equipment and flew to the largely undeveloped area of Daanbantayan on the northernmost end of Cebu Island.

We got our first glimpses of Typhoon Haiyan's impact from the air. Despite the vast destruction that was obvious in every direction, I found the natural scenery of the landscape quite beautiful. The death and destruction from the storm was surrounded by white beaches and coral reefs. Daanbantayan was a popular holiday destination amongst Filipinos and I could see why. I had never been to the Philippines before and my impression was that this would have been a wonderful place for swimming and diving under more favourable circumstances. Obviously there would be none of that on this trip.

Switzerland's ambassador to the Philippines visited Daanbantayan and Bogo, and had meetings with those city's mayors as well as a meeting with Cebu's governor. The ambassador pledged to give the Philippines CHF 6 million in relief aid. The people of Switzerland eventually raised CHF 16 million.

That money was more than welcome but the immediate concern of the survivors was food, water, medicine, shelter. Several countries around the world were offering financial assistance. Monetary donations from private individuals are essential in any disaster recovery. The best humanitarian aid any individual can give is money.

But cash from national governments takes months or even years to go from government to government and trickle down to the people. Nobody has ever held their dead baby in their arms and consoled themselves with the fact that Russia has promised to give their president 50000 euros. Someday.

The biggest difference between aid from one country to another and donations from private citizens is that government money has to filter through several layers of bureaucracy. Political leaders from the countries giving the money have to debate and agree on the details of the aid. When it is finally sent, it then has to wait for political leaders from the recipient country to debate and agree on details of how to use the aid.

Private donations from individuals can go directly from the donor's bank account to the relief organisation's account. There is no need for a quorum or televised press conference.

There was no electricity or water supply when we arrived in northern Cebu. Some food and water had been distributed by the Philippine government but those supplies were all but gone. Oxfam Philippines had delivered hygiene kits and were trying to bring water but they were based in Cebu City and road conditions between Cebu and Daanbantayan, or any areas north of Cebu City, made land travel extremely difficult.

There was also no telephone service anywhere in the area. Conventional telephone lines were all down and cellular signals did not exist. Survivors were just as desperate to communicate with people in other parts of the country as they were for food, water, shelter. At this point everybody had friends and relatives that could have easily been missing or dead. Not being able to contact loved ones in the age of persistent online contact can be disquieting at best.

Bogo was chosen as the Israeli base of operations because it was the kind of area that desperately needed attention but where none of the other delegations or television cameras wanted to go. Most of the news crews were in Tacloban but most of the Visayas were severely affected by the typhoon.

The American delegation insisted on claiming Tacloban whilst Philippine leaders spent most of their time in Cebu City to oversee the arrival of international delegations, and in Tacloban to be seen by the international media. Bogo was an optimal staging ground for rescue operations with ready access to Daanbantayan and Medellin, the nearby islands of Bantayan and Negros, as well as other outlying islands.

The Israeli field hospital was built next to Severo Verallo Memorial District Hospital. This was done because the field hospital was intended as supplementary assistance to the local hospital and to make it easier for local residents to find, as the local hospital was well known in the community. But the Bogo hospital was in no condition to treat hundreds of patients every day. There were only three doctors available and nothing close to enough medicine. They did not have enough space to treat what patients they already had and would never be able to accommodate the thousands more which were on the way.

The longer people had to wait, the worse the overcrowding became. The hospital was running on old generators since there was no electricity in the area. There was insufficient lighting and not even enough power to operate electric fans. Air conditioning was a luxury that would have to wait whilst the outdoor temperature hovered around 30 degrees. It was even hotter inside the crowded acrid building. Coolers full of ice from Cebu City held anything that had to be kept cold.

The staff at Severo Verallo Hospital did as well as they could in such desperate conditions but were understandably overjoyed when the IDF medical teams arrived. The Israeli field hospital would prove to be the only operational medical facility in a region of over 250 000 people.

Daanbantayan was deemed an appropriate landing zone up until the rain brought even more flooding and somebody decided that we should be closer to the field hospital. It rained sporadically the day we arrived and was starting to clear but there had been steady rain

Tuesday and Wednesday. The weather was actually quite nice on some days and was never especially horrible. Other than the massive typhoon before we arrived.

I rather like being outdoors just after a storm. The air is usually cleaner and the atmosphere just feels fresher. Fortunately, most storms are not nearly as destructive as Typhoon Haiyan and the rain that followed was comparatively mild by anybody's definition.

By the time my team arrived at the operations centre in Bogo on Thursday evening most of the delegation were preparing to spend the night in a local sports stadium. The field hospital was almost finished and everybody had worked so hard at getting it put together that no other provisions were made for our housing. I never heard a complaint as we all knew that the hospital was our top priority.

The Don Celestino Martinez Coliseum where we slept that first night had been damaged by the typhoon. It was originally an indoor stadium but after Haiyan it was more or less open air. It also became an impromptu office for Bogo's mayor and city officials as their brand new city hall was destroyed by the typhoon.

A large group of local residents had followed the medical teams as they drove from Cebu City to Bogo. Many of them spent the night with us in the stadium. Most of them had nowhere else to go and I can only assume that other national delegations in other parts of the country were also joined by local survivors.

It almost looked like a war movie where the soldiers carry local children away from their burning village. Except in this case the soldiers did not destroy the village.

Many of the younger children were happy and playing that night but you could tell just by looking at the adults that they had lost everything except whatever they were carrying with them. Most of the parents only had their children and the clothes they were wearing. Some of the parents did not even have their children. About 100 000 people were still unaccounted for at that point. Too many of them were children.

The hospital was not yet complete but the medical teams treated as many people as best they could late into the night. None of this treatment was official. The procedure was to photograph and identify each patient in order to keep accurate medical records. Many of the patients had no form of identification with them. Very few of the Israeli delegation spoke Tagalog or the local Cebu dialect, and I would imagine none of the Filipinos spoke Hebrew.

English is a common second language in both countries but a great deal of information can get lost in translation between a heavy Israeli accent and a heavy Filipino accent. Add the fact that a large percentage of Israelis were born in other countries with other languages and that the Filipinos who came to the field hospital were from a variety of regions and spoke different dialects and you get a true linguistic cacophony. I am almost surprised that everything worked as well as it did.

Without the digital records that were set up the next day it was very difficult to keep track of patient care and little effort was made to categorise and document on that first night. This was mostly triage and first aid treatment. When doctors and nurses are faced with the choice of waiting for the computers to be up and running or treating their patients they tend to go low tech.

I felt about as helpless as possible that first night. My job was to search for some of these missing people but I had to wait until morning. Finding injured people in the middle of catastrophic destruction is difficult enough in high visibility conditions. Dark rainy nights only make everything take longer. Not so much for the aircraft. It does not care about weather or visibility. It is we the people who slow down when tired, wet, and cold.

There were also logistic concerns that needed to be addressed as we had only just arrived in the country. Territorial concerns had to be considered to avoid hurting anybody's feelings.

Put a bunch of adrenaline junkies from a dozen different countries in the middle of a time sensitive operation and you are bound to have a few pissing contests. The Filipinos were officially in charge but representatives from some of the largest and most powerful countries in the world have a tendency to feel more qualified. It was a case of too many cooks in the kitchen and not nearly enough time to keep everything from boiling over.

I had the luxury of not being in charge. Others could determine which delegations could operate in which designated zones. I was in charge of a very small group of people who were far more concerned with evacuating survivors than laying claim to land and air space.

One thing I could do during this negotiation phase was have a look around the field hospital. It was not yet officially open for business but I was still impressed by how much had been accomplished in such a short amount of time.

It was no brick and mortar hospital. It was obviously a temporary structure. But the people who built it and filled it with equipment and supplies clearly knew what they were doing. The command officers at the field hospital had more than enough experience to anticipate what would be needed and how best to accomplish their mission objectives.

That made me feel better. Especially as the enormous scale of destruction I had read about and now seen directly gave me the distinct impression that I was in over my head. Others in our delegation were more than qualified to be here. I was relatively new on the job. My title and responsibilities were commensurate with my years spent with the IDF but my experience with casualty extraction was limited to much smaller scale operations. This was my first nationwide catastrophic event.

My team had penetrated other national

borders and airspace, both at the invitation of those countries and not so much, but we were far more accustomed to evacuating a handful of people and going home. We rarely spent the night in the field of operations and had never faced the possibility that most of the people we were looking for were likely no longer alive.

I told myself that I would have never been sent to the Philippines had the command structure not felt that I was fully capable of leading my team in such a situation. In fact, I would not even have command of such a team of trained professionals without the full confidence of people far more experienced than I. If your performance in the IDF is less than exemplary there are always a dozen people ready to take your place. Those who drop the ball can be and are replaced at a moment's notice. There were 290 people in my bahad tactical flight training class. Six of us graduated.

Part of my job responsibilities require me to exhibit a certain level of confidence. You cannot lead a team whilst telling them that you secretly feel like a little girl doing a woman's job. One of the great benefits of pretending to be confident is that it helps foster actual confidence. I went to the Philippines wondering what I was doing there and left secure in the knowledge that I could lead an entire army to Armageddon.

By the end of the day there were 2537 people confirmed dead, 4053 were injured, and 177 were missing.

My team talked late into the night about everything we had seen and what was yet to come. We had a plan of action and were ready to go. All we needed were the orders from people with higher pay grades. We went to sleep knowing that people were dying outside.

THREE

My team woke up Friday morning before sunrise and headed to our new state of the art cafeteria for breakfast. It was a few folding tables in a corner of the stadium with boxes of packaged food laid out by people who had to wake up even earlier. For the next two weeks there would always be somebody awake somewhere at the hospital.

Some of the other national delegations arrived in large ships. Most of their personnel spent their nights on the same boats where they slept every other night. They never got the full experience of complete immersion. Doing a job in the field and then going back to base every night is a very different experience from living, working, sleeping in the field. I preferred that our delegation spent every minute in the field.

We already knew our mission for the day

and had prepared as much as possible the night before. I submitted my flight plan to our operational headquarters just before I went to sleep Thursday night, insofar as flight plans were used under the circumstances. We had a dedicated airspace and no other organisation was operating flights in our territory. Theoretically.

Commercial air travel in the region was all but nonexistent at this point and other delegations were supposed to stay within their defined territory. The Philippine Civil Aviation Authority did a pretty good job of confining most of their flights farther south to the Mactan-Cebu area.

My team consisted of a flight crew, medical crew, and ground crew. The flight crew were another pilot and me. The medical crew were the flight surgeon and paramedics. The ground crew were maintenance engineers and fuel specialists. We had people from Russia, Canada, Israel, and South Africa. Between us we spoke Hebrew, English, Arabic, Russian, German, Chinese, and Afrikaans. This was a team that could go pretty much anywhere in the world. Yet none of us spoke any of the local Philippine languages besides English.

I was the commanding officer and ostensibly in charge of the team. Nobody in the aircraft has seniority over the pilot in charge. If Buddha, Jesus, and Moses are in that aircraft the pilot in charge is still in charge. The flight surgeon cannot and will not ever tell the pilot how to fly. Just as I would never tell the medical crew how to treat a patient. I am not a doctor and the flight surgeon is not a pilot. But even if we were it would not happen.

The flight surgeon had just been promoted and technically had seniority over me. He was scheduled to transfer to another assignment but volunteered for this operation. We had been working together for almost two years and I was more than happy to have him with us rather than a new replacement. The newest member of the team joined us about a year before Haiyan. We were all accustomed to working together and were a cohesive unit.

This is always best in disaster situations and I have no doubt that it helped all of us do our jobs to the best of our abilities. Anybody who steps into the aircraft is fully qualified and would have been capable of performing their duties. But this would not have been the ideal first mission.

We headed out on a course around the northern tip of Cebu Island, surveying Daanbantayan and Medellin. The southern end of the island reported significantly less damage and was a much lower priority.

The rain had stopped in the middle of the night and it was a clear and beautiful day. We had visibility as far as our eyes could take us. It was as if God opened up the sky for us as soon as we got to work. At least that is what somebody told me. Claiming that God made our day easier only opens the door for more important questions, such as why he brought down on the Philippines such a massive storm in the first place.

People often credit God for getting them out of a horrible situation. I know somebody who will tell any and all that God must surely love him because he was saved from a terrific traffic accident. I tend to point out that if God really loved him then he would have never been in the accident in the first place.

I think it best to leave God out of these issues.

What I assumed would be an IFR pattern on our first survey flight quickly turned to VFR, meaning that we had to rely less on our instruments for visibility. It would have been a great day for a joy ride but we had more pressing things to do.

Daanbantayan was directly in the path of Typhoon Haiyan. To the immediate south is Medellin, over which passed the eye of the typhoon. Both cities suffered catastrophic damage. The reports we received were that 95 to 100 percent of the houses were destroyed. The strongest buildings, the cultural centre, town plaza, municipal hall, were all severely damaged. Most of the private houses were made of far weaker materials and never stood a chance. Almost every single person in the combined population of 125 000 were left homeless.

There was one open road between Cebu City and Bogo, and no roads between Bogo, Medellin, and Daanbantayan. Some of the lower elevation roads were still flooded and most were blocked by debris or too damaged to use. The survivors were waiting for aid but the only way to deliver it was from the air or by boat. Most of the docks were destroyed, making it very difficult for any boats to reach land. Search and rescue teams were the only people coming in by air for the time being.

The mayor of Medellin, Ricardo Ramirez, would later complain that the national government prevented some relief supplies from reaching his city. I have no direct knowledge of that but I know that IDF supplies and private donations from Cebu Island were the only aid reaching local residents during our time there. The national government was supposed to deliver more aid once Israeli infrastructure teams repaired the roads.

Within minutes of taking off from Daanbantayan we spotted a civilian standing in what used to be one of the main roads. There were no other people around him and he made no effort to get our attention. He did not seem to notice us at all. It looked like he was waiting for a bus. Except that there were no buses coming any time soon.

We set down in what was probably a field of some crop or another only a few days earlier. At this point it was just a field. The flight surgeon and one of the paramedics approached the man who did not seem perturbed at all that a military helicopter had just landed in the field across the street. He had no visible injury but was clearly in a state of shock.

We took him to the field hospital and quickly went back out again. Unfortunately, we never found out what he was doing in the street or how long he had been standing there. He was my team's first patient and, although I hate to admit it, we quickly forgot about him as we reached people who were far more seriously injured.

We flew around for a good thirty minutes before we spotted a small group of people frantically trying to get our attention. They were a family of eight with an injured mother and daughter. They all wanted to come with us but there was simply not enough room. None of them spoke English or any of our other languages but we were prepared. We gave them a card with written information in several local languages telling them to stay where they were and that somebody would arrive directly to bring them to the field hospital.

The daughter was severely dehydrated and had minor lacerations on her arms and legs. She was released from the hospital two days later. The mother had impact abdominal trauma and did not survive.

We spent the next five hours flying out to predetermined areas and bringing back as many injured people as we could find. There were more than a few instances where we landed near a population that would have benefited greatly from a shipment of food and water but we were only carrying limited supplies.

We gave our personal supplies of water to groups we found and it did not take long for us to start bringing as much as we could hold every time we went back to the field hospital. But it was never enough. We were essentially first responders and they would have to wait for other teams to help them. The real first responders, of course, were the victims of the typhoon themselves who helped their neighbours and volunteered with local relief efforts.

Since our mission was to evacuate survivors in need of medical treatment we were not staffed to bring relief to the people who needed it the most. A helicopter full of supplies cannot carry injured patients to the hospital. It might seem heartless to walk away from people who desperately need help but our first priority in an emergency situation is medical evacuation.

Other teams were tasked with bringing relief supplies out. My team were responsible for bringing people in. That was our job and that is what we have all been trained to do. We communicated the locations of every group we found, certainly. They were all taken care of in due course. Every man, woman, and child in the area was given food, water, and other supplies by the ground teams. But I personally left a lot of people behind.

The field hospital was still being built when we flew out to survey damage in the morning. By noon it was fully functional. This was no MASH tent. It was an advanced medical facility designed to treat 500 patients a day with departments in pediatrics, obstetrics, casualty and trauma, ambulatory, physiatry, optometry, and an outpatient clinic, staffed with 150 doctors, nurses, technicians under the command of Colonel Dr David Dagan.

The pediatrics department included child psychologists with experience in disaster trauma and a few soldiers whose main job seemed to be handing out thousands of toys to children.

This is why I could never command this kind of operation. I would have thought about the medical equipment and supplies. That much is obvious. I might have thought about rehabilitation and optometry. Maybe. Those departments proved highly useful in Haiti so the people with more experience never gave a second thought to bringing them to the Philippines.

What would have never crossed my mind is bringing toys. They seem superfluous in a disaster recovery operation. To my mind all the space taken up by toys could have held more food and water. But the simple act of giving a child a toy can turn their entire world right way up again.

I tend to focus on the physical aspects of my job and often disregard the psychological. But there is as much emotional suffering in the wake of a massive disaster as there is physical. Children are especially susceptible to psychological distress since it is much harder for them to understand why their homes and schools have violently disappeared. It is also much harder for them to coherently express their anguish. A child psychologist can be just as important as a surgeon.

Whilst my team were out and about we missed visits to the field hospital by both Bogo Mayor Junie Martinez and Philippines Vice President Jejomar Binay, whose wife is a doctor. Far more importantly, the first of many babies was born that day. The happy parents named him Israel.

I personally would never name a child after a country. But if I had to I would choose Djibouti.

After a quick lunch at the hospital we were back out in the field. From the air we could see heart breaking scenes of devastation on the ground juxtaposed with the island's natural beauty. There were collapsed houses and hotels next to white sandy beaches. Fallen palm trees covering roofless schools. The remains of a hospital littered with the decimated crops of a nearby field. We saw boats washed ashore, some much farther inland than a boat has any right to be.

We came upon a small group of people swimming in an area that was still flooded. We assumed that these people were not swimming for recreation and transported them to dry land. None of them were injured so we gave them our water and were on our way.

Most of the flood water had already receded but there were still small lakes in places where no lake existed a week before. This is an area that lies just above sea level, with some inland depressions below sea level. The water from massive tidal waves can take weeks to subside when the sky is mostly cloudy.

Recovery efforts were moving very slowly at this point and everybody's main concern was locating survivors and delivering supplies. Cleaning and rebuilding would come much later.

Even hazardous debris was mostly ignored. A ship that was anchored off Iloilo before the typhoon struck was damaged enough to cause a major oil spill along the coast and in the surrounding sea. The oil spill was not under control until Friday; a week after the storm. It has still not been fully cleaned to date.

By the end of the day my team had made a dozen flights back to the field hospital with people needing medical attention, and too many flights back without anybody. The hospital treated 140 patients that day and all of our search and rescue teams located 62 people. We were making ourselves useful but we knew that our efforts would only help a tiny fraction of the country's needs. At that point 1 871 321 people were homeless because of Haiyan.

Throughout the country 375 795 people were given water, rice, canned food, and biscuits. Some news reporter asked why they were given biscuits, as if people were being given cake when they had no bread. Biscuits are a common disaster relief staple. They provide protein, calcium, and a lot of other vitamins and minerals in an easy to deliver and eat package.

Much of the Israeli delegation went to Haiti in 2010. They had experience with disaster on this scale. My team were experienced in individual casualty extraction. The massive devastation of Typhoon Haiyan was new to us and we were still getting used to how bad things were here. And we knew that it was only going to get worse.

At the end of our day all the patients were receiving treatment, the equipment was safe and secure, reports and logs were filed. Much of the medical personnel were still working in the field hospital when my team went to sleep. I stayed awake longer than I probably should have and looked around the hospital. It was far busier than the previous night. Before the hospital officially opened it was like a clinic in the middle of the night. Now it was just like any other hospital. Medical treatment does not care what time it is. As busy as it was I knew that it was only going to get busier.

I went to sleep thinking about everything. I thought about what we saw and did that day, and about what might come tomorrow. I thought about what would happen to my own country in such an enormous disaster. Watching the pain and suffering of people you know little about is horrible enough. Watching my friends and family endure such devastation would be unimaginably horrific. I thought about all the people we had seen and those we would inevitably see in the coming days. Mostly I thought about all the people that we would never find. Thousands of parents, children, siblings, friends were missing. Many would never be seen again.

A certain level of emotional detachment is required whilst I am on duty. You simply cannot empathise with people during their darkest moments and complete the task at hand. It would be like a surgeon who is afraid to cut people. Sometimes you have to be willing to amputate their limbs to save their lives. But when the day is done and your head hits that dreadfully inadequate military surplus pillow it is almost impossible to keep all of those suppressed emotions at bay. I would doubt that anybody in this profession is thoroughly indifferent to the suffering of others. It would not only make it difficult to do a job that requires helping others but it would also make it difficult to be human.

I fell asleep knowing that thousands of people in the immediate vicinity would not be sleeping at all.

We woke up to rain on Saturday morning but we were no less eager to get on with our mission. In fact, the rain brought a greater sense of urgency. We always knew there were more people out there and this latest patch of rain did not help them at all. It was not an especially heavy rain but more people died because of it.

Saturday's rainfall made transport between Daanbantayan and Bogo more difficult than necessary. An argument can be made, and was made more than a few times, that the landing zone should have always been closer to the field hospital. But the last thing you want to do is land some helicopters right next to a temporary hospital where you expect to receive a constant flood of patients coming and going in every direction.

We spent most of the morning relocating the landing zone instead of looking for survivors. This was a waste of time to my mind but the damage was done and corrected. We were all more interested in doing our jobs in the present than complaining about how mistakes could have been avoided in the past.

By the time my team went out on our first flight of the day there were well over 200 people queued at the hospital. People travelled from all corners of Cebu Island and from much of the Visayas. Those who could were finding their way to us. It was our turn to bring in those who could not.

From our new landing zone we got a terrific view of the field hospital and all the people waiting patiently for treatment. I was impressed by how well the people of the Philippines handled themselves in such a horrible situation. Aside from the looting just after the storm there was almost no crime or violence. The government may or may not have been in a state of anarchy but the people remained civilised. It reminded me of the Japanese people after the 2011 Fukushima earthquake and tsunami. They retained their dignity in the face of staggering death and destruction.

From the air we could also see more people making their way to the hospital. Most were on foot but some were being pushed in trolleys and anything else that could carry a person on wheels.

It was going to be a busy day.

My team spent most of the afternoon locating and identifying people in Bogo and Medellin. This is both a necessary process and very aggravating at the same time. It means the world to any disaster victim to see other people and be told that food is coming but others were dying whilst we were doing this. We all knew that every minute we talked to people who were uninjured was another minute not giving medical aid to somebody in desperate need. As many search and rescue teams as there were from as many countries that sent them it simply was not enough.

Five million children were affected by Typhoon Haiyan. Of those 5 million, 1.5 million were under the age of five and most vulnerable to the harsh conditions and lack of medical care. Three million people were still homeless on Saturday and 371 000 were living in 1086 evacuation centres. The latest reports were that 12501 people were injured, 1186 were missing, 3631 were confirmed dead. We all went through every range of emotions humans can feel throughout our mission but the sheer volume of destruction was overwhelming.

The best thing you can do in this situation is to soldier on. We had no idea if our efforts were having any effect but we knew we had a job to do.

We picked up a few people with serious injuries but most were minor. The most difficult part of the day was turning away people who just wanted somewhere to go. We gave them information about the field hospital and evacuation centres or gave directions to their location to other teams that could better help them. But my team essentially did nothing for them.

During our last flight of the day we spotted a small fixed wing aircraft resting uncomfortably on a street, field, and in what used to be a house about 100 metres from the field. We knew that nobody could have possibly survived the crash but we had to investigate it anyway. Most of the fuselage was on what used to be a street. There was no pilot or passenger alive or dead inside. We briefly considered that they might have survived the crash and made their way to safety.

That theory lasted about a minute before we found most of a body inside the remains of the house. He had been dead for at least a week.

The Philippines is a tropical environment and this was still the rainy season. Combine heat with humidity and rotting flesh and you get a banquet for insects and their larvae. It is not pretty.

Some of another body was found in the shredded field. It was the first time I had ever seen a severed head that was not the result of terrorism. From the distance of the wreckage and remains it was later determined that the aircraft was in flight during the typhoon and torn apart prior to descent.

We had to leave the remains and alert another team. Had we transported every dead body we found we would have never had time to evacuate the living.

Corpses were piling up all over the Visayas, creating a serious health hazard. Especially when people were drinking flood water that was contaminated with dead humans, dead animals, raw sewage, and all manner of debris. Cholera and salmonella were serious concerns. As were infected injuries since most people had no clean water to drink let alone with which to bathe. It was not until the following week that a concerted effort was made to remove the dead.

When we went to sleep that night I felt about as useless as a vegan at Oktoberfest. We heard reports of people doing all manner of good work all over the region.

The Americans, Japanese, Australians were saving lives left, right, and centre. The Israeli hospital treated 370 patients that day, including 150 children. Saturday was also the first full day that the optometry department was fully functional and doctors had use of the laboratory and x-rays.

More children were being successfully delivered. For some of the mothers it was the first visit of their pregnancy to a hospital. For others it was their first hospital visit ever.

Yet I personally did almost nothing. Rain does not usually make me depressed but on that rainy day surrounded by so many torn and broken souls and finding so many dead bodies

I was not at my most cheerful.

Some of the Israeli delegation liked to spend time in the maternity and pediatric departments. Smiling happy children have a way of cheering people up. I found it all rather depressing. The children may have been happy in the moment but I could only think about how many of them lost their parents and how difficult it will be as they struggle to cope with what has happened.

Long after all of us foreigners have gone home these people will still be rebuilding their lives.

I was there to evacuate injured survivors. I spent half of the day dealing with bureaucracy. We located plenty of uninjured people, which is not at all depressing, but the ground teams could have easily done that. Bogo, Medellin, and Daanbantayan are all on the same island. Ground teams could reach all of them once the roads were cleared. My team could go where others could not and we were being restricted to a limited area by publicity seekers and diplomacy.

Each country was in charge of its own operations within a limited framework set by the Philippine government. It would probably be far better if we could all work together and combine our efforts but getting a hundred different countries to agree on how to do anything is the closest thing there is to impossible.

British military ships patrolled the waters north of our designated island. Chinese ships were to the south. To the west of us were the Canadians and to the east were the Australians. We were surrounded by people who generally like us. More or less. But when you have military personnel from a dozen different countries in a relatively small area it is often best to keep your distance.

The American and Chinese delegations, or possibly the Philippine government, made sure there were large islands separating their forces. It would have been extremely difficult for them to casually bump into each other. My team were restricted to a small area that would have received attention whether we were there or not.

Looking around, I could see great room for improvement. But in a situation such as this it is often best to do your job and hope that everybody else is doing theirs.

My immediate concern was the people who were stuck between one area of responsibility and another. Nobody was taking care of them. I went to the Philippines to help these people. I was not there to debate jurisdiction or political ministrations. I went to sleep with every intention to change this as much as I possibly could.

FOUR

Sunday morning started with an early meeting before breakfast. The senior commander of the Home Front Command National Search and Rescue Unit, Colonel Ramtin Sabti, felt the same way as I did about how best to achieve our mission objective for perhaps the first time in the history of the universe. When I was thinking of how to complain about the way we were doing things, he and his command officers were finding a better way to do things. Maybe they thought of it sooner. All that mattered was that my team were going to be more useful from here on.

"About zdayen time," I said when we were briefed. Some people still wonder why it takes me so long to get promoted.

I went over our addended mission strategy with the rest of my team over breakfast. Everybody was just as eager as I was to act more like paramedics than police officers, especially the actual paramedics on the team.

It should probably be noted that my complaints about our dawdling pace are only applicable to my team and perhaps one or two of the other search and rescue teams. The medical staff at the field hospital did nothing but good, day and night, from the time we arrived until we left. The infrastructure teams accomplished more in days than most of the people on some of the smaller islands had seen in their lifetime.

It should be noted because I get myself in enough trouble already.

My team flew 65 kilometres over the Visayan Sea to Negros Island on Sunday. CNN, BBC, and other international media were all talking about Tacloban, the capital of Leyte Province. Leyte Island in the Eastern Visayas was indeed heavily damaged with thousands of people killed but most of the international delegations were based in or near Leyte. Those people were getting the help they needed.

Over 70 percent of the Philippines' homeless were on the Western Visayas islands of Negros and Panay, with most of the damage in the Aklan, Antique, Iloilo provinces of Panay Island, and cities on the north end of Negros Island. The Canadian delegation were based in Iloilo and taking care of most of Panay Island. Negros was being ignored.

The full force of the typhoon hit the northern tip of Negros, taking away most of the houses. My team went to Cadiz, the farthest city north on the island and the most heavily affected. Cadiz is a farming and fishing city of just over 150 000 people. An estimated 80 percent of the city's buildings were destroyed.

Yet they did not need us in Cadiz. There were few fatalities and most of those injured were already receiving medical attention by the time we arrived. Apparently the local government did a very good job with warnings before Typhoon Haiyan hit. Most of the people who lived in weaker houses went to designated evacuation centres.

What the city needed most when we arrived was electricity and reconstruction. The electricity was intermittent but available more often than in other areas. The biggest complaint I heard during our very brief time there was a lack of phone service. This can be very important when you are trying to contact loved ones but it was never within the purview of my team.

To the immediate east of Cadiz is Sagay, a smaller city in a similar situation. Buildings and agriculture were heavily damaged but there were few serious injuries and no reported fatalities. Residents had been evacuated prior to the typhoon's impact. They needed food, water, shelter, electricity, and everything else that my team could not provide. Beyond that, everybody was present and accounted for and none needed to be rescued. Other teams would provide for their needs in the near future.

Sagay is mostly known for its marine reserves that are actively reforesting the area's natural mangroves. The reserves are the city's main tourist attraction with much of the money spent by tourists going back into preservation activities which, in turn, generates more interest in tourism. The mangroves returned the favour by protecting most of Sagay from the 5 metre waves that would have otherwise caused far more serious damage and more fatalities.

Mangrove forests were also native to parts of Samar and Leyte before being destroyed years ago as those areas were developed. Many of the deaths in the Eastern Visayas could have been prevented had the mangroves still existed.

People often ask why nature wants to kill humans so much. Maybe if we destroyed a little less of it we would have more natural protection from events like typhoons and floods.

I have never doubted the strength of a flourishing mangrove forest but after seeing the direct result of a massive typhoon impact on other cities and islands I would have assumed that these mangroves were no more. Whilst flying overhead we could see almost no evidence that the mangroves were even in the storm's path. Houses, trees, fields were torn to debris but the mangroves survived fully intact. Even the vast destruction of the world's largest typhoon impact is not enough to take down flourishing mangroves. It takes the vast destruction of man.

The northern end of Negros Island suffered major damage. Upwards of 50000 houses were destroyed. Thousands of commercial and public buildings were seriously damaged. Anything not fastened to the Earth was uprooted, as were countless trees and farms. But very few people on the island were killed. Most of the injuries were minor.

Everybody we met was more concerned with locating friends and relatives in other parts of the country. Local governments and the island's provincial governor evacuated more than 60000 people before Typhoon Haiyan made landfall. Their efforts deserve a great deal of credit. As do the mangroves.

My team were supposed to spend the day on Negros Island assessing the situation, locating survivors, and evacuating casualties. Reports of massive damage on northern Negros led our command to believe that we would be there for at least two days. I made the decision to cease operations on the island before lunch. Other teams would obviously send aid and all manner of relief supplies and equipment but we aborted all search and rescue efforts on the island.

My team spent the rest of the day in the Cebu Island areas of Daanbantayan, Medellin, and Bogo. I had complained far and wide that we should be allowed to search areas beyond Cebu Island yet I was the one who decided to abort our plans on Negros and return to Cebu. The irony was not lost on me nor any of my team. They still remind me of it to this day.

Everybody agreed that it was the right decision. There is little point in sending search and rescue teams to an island without any missing or unattended people. But a group of highly trained professionals who work closely with each other every day inside a small levitating box cannot and should not pass any opportunity to ridicule a colleague.

You are never part of a team if that team cannot mock you.

The Israeli field hospital treated 582 patients on Sunday, including 244 children, and delivered three babies in the space of one hour. The Philippines had an oddly high number of pregnant women when Typhoon Haiyan hit and many of them gave birth in horrible conditions. Some had their children in overcrowded evacuation centres. A few were lucky enough to deliver in the Israeli or Australian field hospitals. Too many babies were born in the rubble where houses once stood.

The Israeli field hospital was originally designed to treat 500 patients a day but it did not take long before everybody realised that it would have to be able to do more before it could eventually do less.

The infrastructure teams built a water filtration system and cistern on Gibitngil Island to provide the people clean drinking water for the first time in nine days.

Ground teams spent the day locating and transporting survivors, and delivering desperately needed aid to much of Cebu Island.

None of this was a competition. Far from it. But once again I ended my day with the distinct impression that everybody else in the country was doing far more than I was.

Sunday's reports had 3976 people confirmed dead, 15718 were injured, and 1590 people were still missing.

It rained pretty much without interruption on Monday 18 November. This was the end of the rainy season but it was not ready to end just yet. In spite or because of the rain it would also prove to be the field hospital's single busiest day.

My team flew 35 kilometres to Bantayan Island. This was a small island with a population of just under 150 000. There were no TV news crews here. There was also no fishing industry as there had been before the typhoon. Bantayan Island supplied most of the fish for Cebu and Negros. It was also one of the largest sources of eggs for the entire Visayas. Typhoon Haiyan put an end to that.

Bantayan Island was directly in the path of the storm and pretty much decimated. Chris Escario, the mayor of the city of Bantayan, said that the island looked like a war zone. And it did. I have seen actual war zones with more standing buildings and more signs of life. Initial estimates were that up to 95 percent of the island's houses had no roofs. Well over 70 percent were no more than piles of rubble. There was no electricity anywhere on the island and the fresh water supply was completely cut off. The Philippine government did not expect to restore electricity service for several months. Clean water would not be available until IDF infrastructure teams installed new water systems in the following days.

The municipal hall in Bantayan was used as an evacuation centre but far too small to handle the waves of people coming in every day. There was a tourist centre three times larger across the street but it was made with weaker materials than the municipal hall's concrete and far too unstable to house survivors.

The Bantayan gymnasium was designated as an evacuation centre before the storm but lost part of its roof when the typhoon tore apart the island. Despite the damage, it became home to thousands of people from Bantayan Island and smaller surrounding islands.

Most roads were impassable and even the open roads were littered with heavy debris. Local aid workers reported that land travel between Santa Fe and Bantayan nine kilometres away took anywhere from 45 to 60 minutes where before the typhoon it took 10 minutes at most.

This island is no stranger to typhoons but the people we met all told us that Yolanda brought far and away the most destruction they had ever seen. We also never came across a single person who did not lose at least one family member in the typhoon. Many of them had no surviving relatives. Far too many had no idea where some of their loved ones were.

People were talking about Yolanda. I initially had no idea who that was. Whereas the rest of the world called the typhoon Haiyan it was called Yolanda in the Philippines. Fair enough. If a typhoon tears apart your country and kills thousands of people you can call it whatever you want.

Relief efforts on Bantayan Island before we arrived were being coordinated by Gail Roska. She was not with any of the international delegations. She did not even work for any department or agency of the Philippines. She was simply a civilian living on Cebu Island who wanted to help.

She and countless other volunteers like her that most of the international media will never know about were responsible for most of the relief efforts in Central and Western Visayas before Israel, Canada, China, Britain, other international delegations finally made their way to the Philippines.

The world was focused on Tacloban but the people of Bantayan were also dying. Relief was slow to arrive and difficult to deliver. It took several long days after the typhoon for any international aid to reach the Philippines and all levels of the government were beyond overwhelmed.

Bantayan Island was completely isolated from initial relief efforts because of large coastal waves following the typhoon. Local volunteers did not have the luxury of helicopters, leaving boats as the only source of transportation to the island.

Habitat for Humanity Philippines sent 29 volunteers from Cebu City over the weekend with 500 emergency shelter kits donated by

Habitat for Humanity Great Britain. The shelter kits allowed people to put temporary roofs over whatever standing buildings they had or use them as tents if their homes were reduced to rubble. They are far from permanent housing but better than sleeping in the rain by night and exposed to the harsh sunlight by day.

The people on Bantayan Island had no relief from the elements with almost no intact roofs on the island and very few standing trees to provide shade. With a practically steady stream of rain it was easy to forget that when the sun was out it was unforgiving to people without homes or trees for protection.

Even after supplies arrived, much of it waited for a week or more in Manila and Cebu City to be delivered to outlying islands. The nation's infrastructure was severely damaged. There were not enough trucks to move supplies to the docks and not enough boats to get to the islands. What little ground transportation they had was delayed by blocked and broken roads. We will never know how many people died because the aid they needed was sitting in a warehouse or on an airfield.

People like Gail Roska were the only relief for most Filipinos in the immediate aftermath of the storm. She and her family collected donations of food and water from Cebu and brought them by boat to Bantayan Island as soon as sea conditions were stable enough to make the crossing. They were soon receiving donations from every corner of the Philippines and eventually from around the world. By the time we arrived they were also delivering blankets, tents, and whatever medicine they could get.

In a fair world, Gail Roska and people like her would get more press than whatever sociopath is shooting up an American school this month. I have never understood why we turn murderers into celebrities and ignore people who actually help their fellow man. The fact that a typical humanitarian does not want fame while the typical serial killer wants to be a superstar says something about the nature of celebrity.

Monday was a busy day for my team. After we assessed the situation on the ground we flew around the perimeter of Bantayan Island and surveyed the damage. One of the prominent fishing villages was on the western shore of the island. Most of those boats had completely disappeared. Typhoon Haiyan moved from east to west and took almost everything in the water with it. A few boats were still there on top of collapsed roofs and inside the debris of buildings. We found a fishing boat two kilometres inland near the road to the tiny domestic airport. The airport itself was heavily damaged.

There was unending destruction in every direction but our initial reports said that the heaviest damage was in the central region of Bantayan Island. It was easy to agree. From the air it looked like the island had been carpet bombed. There were even small impact craters from uprooted groves of trees. The only good news was that most of the island was undeveloped. The typhoon destroyed a great many trees and empty fields along with all the homes and farms. The bad news was that there were tiny villages spread out all across the island. Getting to all of them would take a long time.

We found a young man crawling in one of the obliterated farms. He was cradling something in his arms. From the air it looked like an assault rifle; in both its shape and the way he was holding it. This presented us with a unique situation.

Obviously we had to land and investigate. Even people who walked upright and appeared uninjured required identification and, almost exclusively, were grateful for whatever information we could provide. Anybody crawling on the ground had our full attention.

But his apparent weapon was problematic. Survivors in the aftermath of a massive disaster are often in shock. They are commonly capable of acting in a manner that is counterintuitive to their survival. Any unidentifiable person with a weapon is a potential threat in the best of circumstances. Conditions in this situation were not ideal.

My team are trained military officers. We were armed and fully capable of defending ourselves should such a need arise. But the last thing we were authorised to do during search and rescue operations was to fire on a civilian who was clearly in distress. If we landed at his position and he fired on us then our only option would be to secure the aircraft and create a distance between us and him. Military police would have to be sent to his location and somebody would likely be injured or killed.

My support pilot and I analysed the situation for about a second before determining that we had to land. We alerted the medical crew to the possibility of weapons fire and set down near the crawling man.

Our concerns were prudent but unfounded. The man was not holding a weapon. It was his severed leg. He had crawled a not unimpressive distance across the field whilst tightly gripping his former limb. It was like a scene out of a Steven Spielberg movie.

He was taken immediately to the field hospital where he was treated and fully expected to recover. There was never any possibility of reattaching his limb since it had spent well over a week in a humid and highly septic environment without any blood flow or so much as a single ice cube.

It may be little consolation to this young man but he was fortunate to be found by people with advanced medical equipment. He was treated by doctors who were able to give him a prosthesis that was fitted specifically to his needs. Had he been treated by local personnel he would have likely been left with a rudimentary artificial limb or simply a stump.

National delegations such as Israel and Canada were able to bring all manner of comprehensive treatment to the Philippines.

Local medical centres and personnel were simply overwhelmed.

My team made eight trips back to the field hospital with eleven serious to critical patients. We located 39 survivors and gave information about the field hospital and the Bantayan evacuation centre to countless others.

We also tagged more dead bodies than I care to remember. No effort was being made at this point to clear the dead on Bantayan Island. It was impossible to move more than a few kilometres on the ground without running into a dead body. Rotting corpses were in the middle of streets and in collapsed houses where their families slept. People were keeping their dead relatives with them because they had nowhere else to place them and nowhere else to go.

My team only reluctantly ended our day after the sun set. We were prohibited from flying two hours after dusk. Specifically, two hours after the sun reached 18 degrees below the horizon. Somebody once asked me how we know when the sun is at 18 degrees. My answer was that we are Israeli. We know.

A more accurate explanation is that our navigation systems know our precise longitude, latitude, altitude, bearing at any given point in time and can tell us the corresponding location of the sun in relation to our position. I personally know precious little about the declination of the sun on a good day but the aircraft knows all.

Bogo from the air looked like any other

small city at night. There were lights from the field hospital and a small cluster in the distance over Cebu City. There was sporadic electricity on Cebu Island but some of the southern areas were always lit at night.

Bantayan Island was completely dark at night. From the air it was a black spot in the reflective sea. The entire island's electric service was down. There was no light to speak of before generators were brought in. There is something eerie in looking at an island of over one hundred thousand people trying to survive in total darkness.

The Sikorsky UH-60 is fully operational at night and can be flown just as well in zero visibility as it can on a crystal clear day. The personnel locator system has infrared and night vision capabilities that can find a survivor on the ground at night far easier than anybody can spot a person with the naked eye in broad daylight.

The days of sticking your head out the window to look for people are long gone. With today's technology you can spot a person lying in their bed under heavy blankets in the ground floor apartment of a ten storey building from a helicopter 4000 metres above ground level. It is more than a little impressive and frightening at the same time.

We could have easily looked for survivors at night but everybody has to sleep sooner or later. People smarter than I decided that all search and rescue teams should operate in daylight hours rather than stagger shifts and risk clearing a search grid when survivors might have been missed. The difference between night and day is more about the operator than the aircraft.

There is also the very real issue of safety and security. We are more visible to the people on the ground in the daylight. Our aircraft can operate in a pitch black lightning storm but it can also operate on a calm sunny day. It simply made sense to work in the daytime.

All of the discussions about visibility and conditions were moot once the weather went from bad to worse.

Our orders were to report back to Bogo for lunch every day. That might seem gratuitous under the circumstances but proper nutrition and hydration are essential with any teams negotiating in the field and any substantial distance from their base of operations.

Bringing your lunch presents safety issues. Flying over the ocean in a twelve tonne ambulance filled with 3000 pounds of jet fuel is not a picnic. As much as it perturbs most of my team I put safety above all other considerations. This is not a movie where being criminally reckless is rewarded and people get out of impossible situations at the last second without suffering any consequences.

There is also the issue of aircraft maintenance. The best way to destroy a turbine engine is to push it beyond its limits. The last thing you want to do is search and rescue a search and rescue team. We had enough problems with that later on.

That said, we decided to forgo our mandatory lunch break. We all agreed that there was simply too much to do. We had a hearty breakfast and adequate dinner every day. Lunch we could live without. I decided that if we were questioned and/or reprimanded for ignoring our orders I would say that I gave my team no choice in the matter. They have no control over where the aircraft goes. But I never bothered to tell my team any of this until after the fact.

My plan was to blatantly lie to my commanding officer and say that we had sufficient rest and nutrition during the day. We were bringing small amounts of food and water for the locals every time we flew to Bantayan Island anyway. It would not have been impossible for us to eat some of that food and take a break somewhere outside of Bogo.

It was a minor infraction but one that could have consequences. My team felt strongly enough that we were all more than willing to ignore our orders. But I was not about to let any of them pay the price. I would go home and let a replacement take command of my team if necessary but I was not going to allow anything to happen to them.

It was an obvious choice and one that took me a fraction of a second to make. Anything less would be tantamount to cowardice. Any leader who does not take responsibility for their team is not much of a leader and has no business being in command in the first place.

Anybody who has watched Jimmy Stewart movies knows that. I was ready, willing, and able to listen to a lecture on how regulations must be followed for the good of the unit.

It did not work out that way. After our final landing of the day I had a meeting with my commanding officer. He either had no idea that we ignored our orders or, more likely, he chose not to worry about it. There are regulations in hopefully every country in the world dictating the amount of rest a pilot must have before any amount of time spent in control of the aircraft. There are also times when judgement on the ground, or in the air, must supersede edicts written on paper.

The field hospital treated 952 patients on Monday. Far more than the 500 a day that it was designed to treat. People came from areas of the Philippines far and wide once word spread of an Israeli hospital that was treating anybody and everybody without charge. The health care and health cover systems in the Philippines can be exceptional for those with enough wealth. Poorer areas of the country have fewer hospitals and far fewer doctors. Some populated islands have no access to health care whatsoever.

Many of the patients treated at the field hospital had never seen a doctor before. Some had chronic conditions such as diabetes, cancer, HIV. A few patients had cancerous tumours removed on the same day that they were diagnosed.

The mission of the field hospital was to

treat survivors of the typhoon but its purpose was to treat anybody who required medical attention. Whether their conditions were the result of the storm or not was irrelevant.

Outside of the hospital, infrastructure teams rebuilt a local school. Reopening the schools was a priority for local government officials and they specifically asked for Israel's assistance before the first team hit the ground. Monday was the first day of classes. Some of the Israeli delegation substituted for teachers who were otherwise occupied because of the typhoon.

Those must have been some interesting classes.

Roughly 837 900 packages of food were delivered throughout the country. Some of the survivors had not eaten a full mean since before the typhoon. There were 4011 people confirmed dead, with 18175 injured, and 1602 missing.

FIVE

It was raining when we woke on Tuesday morning. There was nothing particularly dramatic about it but we knew that it would likely rain the entire day. This was nothing the people on Bantayan Island needed.

Ground teams used our reconnaissance from the previous day whilst my team went to more isolated areas. We located more survivors and brought more patients to the field hospital on Tuesday than on any other day. It astounded me to see how many people were still waiting for rescue eleven days after the typhoon.

Bantayan Island is a popular holiday spot for its beautiful white beaches and clean tropical shore. It is the kind of place that some people would describe as a tropical paradise. More so before the typhoon than after.

We found a man with both ankles broken

on an isolated beach literally praying for somebody to find him. His injuries were not life threatening but he could not move himself away from the beach. He lived off of whatever small sea animals crawled next to him, and spent every night fully exposed to the elements for eleven long days.

He cried when we found him and told us that we were angels sent in answer to his prayers. I think if he got to know us a little better he would have reconsidered that assessment.

Everybody was grateful to see us. We heard the word "salamat" in various forms more than anything else. But I started to feel guilty about how long it took to reach them.

I was the person in distress myself following an incident in 2002 under very different circumstances. The weather was favourable and I had enough food to last for days. I was found in under twelve hours. Far less time than it took us to find survivors in the Philippines.

I knew how happy I was to see the people who found me in less than a day, so I could completely understand what the survivors we found after a week were feeling.

Each person we located had a story of survival to tell. Some of them were too horrible to remember. Too many of them were too horrible to forget. All of the time we wasted on plans and preparations, moving things from here to there, organising and reorganising meant that injured people would have to wait that much longer for medical treatment.

The medical teams did a pretty amazing job, all things considered. And all of those advanced preparations made it possible to help as many people as we did in the most efficient way possible. The field hospital treated its thousandth patient on Tuesday. But when you look at somebody who has been dying in a field or who delivered their own baby in the middle of the street it is hard to ignore the fact that we could have reached them sooner.

Even worse are the dead bodies that you know were alive the day before. Had we turned left instead of right, done that instead of this, those people would be alive today. The sobering counter argument is that some of the people we helped would have died had we gone another way.

The people we helped called us heroes. There was never a single moment that I agreed with them. The heroes were the Filipinos who put their own recovery on hold to help out their neighbours. I and my team did our job. We did what we get paid to do. The locals who left their jobs and homes to help strangers on other islands did it because it had to be done.

Nobody did more for the Philippines than the people of the Philippines themselves. Despite losing their own homes, farms, businesses, we saw Filipino volunteers practically everywhere we went. Filipinos have become accustomed to helping their neighbours after a natural disaster with collective action known locally as bayanihan.

They help each other not for praise or glory but because it is the right thing to do. Such an attitude is always for the best but even more convenient in this instance because most of the relief workers were never noticed by the media.

By Tuesday 19 November, eleven days after the typhoon, international media crews were all but gone. It was the biggest story in the world on 9 November, and all the journalists were telling us what a great job they did covering the relief efforts on 12 November. They all started leaving as soon as the international delegations arrived and were mostly out of the country within a week. Death and destruction probably gets higher ratings than relief and recovery. There were 4.4 million homeless people in the Philippines but they were apparently not worth the ratings.

I think this is why the media crews lasted longer in Haiti. Rescue operations took a very long time in Haiti and the recovery was very slow. The country is still recovering with thousands of people living in temporary shelters at present.

Either that or because Haiti is in North America and the Philippines is only in Asia. CNN's priorities are the United States, Canada, Europe, the rest of North America, and then everybody else. BBC is similar except that they put Europe first, then the United States, Commonwealth states, and then everybody else.

I do not complain that an American news corporation puts the United States first or that a British corporation puts Britain first. I simply feel that if you want to call yourself an international news organisation then you should probably recognise that there are more than twelve countries in the world.

I also think the complete lack of news cameras made it easier for us to do our jobs. The American delegation had to contend with reporters and photographers amidst their rescue and recovery mission. Finding dead bodies is hard enough without somebody shoving a camera in your face and asking you how you feel about it.

I have nothing but sympathy for our American counterparts. They did a difficult job under difficult circumstances and had to contend with celebrity journalists who care more about their image and what kind of award they might get than they do about what is happening to the suffering people around them. And the Americans did their job with the utmost professionalism and composure. As far as I know.

But it was interesting to compare reports by international reporters with those by Filipino reporters. CNN and BBC at first criticised local governments in their handling of the storm whilst local reporters offered praise. The international news agencies started blaming the national government when the national government said that local officials were preoccupied with their own problems since they were also victims of the typhoon.

Filipino reports were that relief efforts

started a little slower than everybody would have liked but that their elected officials were doing the best they could in extreme conditions.

Then the international and local forces turned on each other. ABS-CBN reporter Korina Sanchez said that CNN reporter Anderson Cooper had no idea what he was talking about after he complained about relief reaching the people too slowly. Not so much because anything he reported was factually inaccurate but because he was a foreigner with blond hair. I always thought he had grey hair but Korina Sanchez said otherwise.

Other Filipinos were quick to point out that Sanchez is married to a national politician who will likely run for president in 2016. She had a personal stake in how the international media portrayed the Filipino government.

For his part, Cooper simply invited Sanchez to get out of Manila and visit the devastation in Tacloban as he himself had done.

This celebrity bickering was either a welcome diversion from the day's events or horribly inappropriate given the climate of death and suffering in which it occurred. Depending on your point of view.

We never saw anything about it on the nightly news but the Israeli delegation made clean water available to all of Cebu Island by Tuesday. New filtration systems were installed every day until the entire island had access to potable water.

Other teams delivered thousands of meals to villages throughout northern Cebu Island and Negros Island. The Canadian delegation were doing the same thing on Panay Island. None of that was on the news either. In fact, from the news reports it would be easy to assume that only the islands of Leyte and Samar were affected by Typhoon Haiyan, and that the United States was the only country to send any humanitarian aid to the Philippines. All of the people we met felt otherwise.

News reporters generally seem more concerned with how they look on camera and getting a story that might win some kind of award that is only prestigious to them but what they tell their audience can make an enormous difference.

The people of the United States give more charitable contributions than anyone else on the planet. People can argue all day about economic advantage and religious influence but the statistics show that Americans, in general, will give to others in their time of need.

Americans donated more money after Hurricanes Katrina and Sandy not simply because those storms were in the United States but also because each storm received demonstrably greater media coverage than Typhoon Haiyan. By ignoring Haiyan after the first week, the international media denied the people of the Philippines exposure to those who may have been more willing and able to help.

None of this is surprising given that most countries will pay more attention to events that take place within their borders than to events on the other side of the globe. At the same time, humans tend to help each other no matter where we live as long as we know that people need help. Most Americans, and indeed most of the world, likely never had any idea just how enormous the scale of destruction was in the Philippines.

Hurricane Katrina hit the southern United States in 2005. It is arguably the most famous cyclone in the world. Mostly because of extensive international media coverage. The storm was about 400 miles in diameter with wind speeds up to 155 miles per hour.

Hurricane Sandy hit the eastern United States in 2012. It was about 940 miles in diameter with winds up to 115 miles per hour, and the largest storm ever recorded in the Atlantic Ocean, though less famous internationally than Katrina.

Typhoon Haiyan is already mostly forgotten outside of southeast Asia. It was over 1200 miles in diameter with winds up to 235 miles per hour when it impacted the Philippines, according to the US Joint Typhoon Warning Center. Had it hit the United States it could have covered Nova Scotia to Mexico. It would have also been the single largest news story in the history of the world.

People will say that Katrina and Sandy each cost more money than Haiyan. Katrina caused US$125 billion in damages, making it one of the most expensive natural disasters ever recorded, whilst Sandy caused US$68 billion. Haiyan was a mere US$14 billion.

But everything in the United States is more expensive than in the Philippines. The average house on Long Island is going to cost far more to replace than the average house on Bantayan Island.

In context, Katrina cost 0.8 percent of US gross domestic product. Sandy was 0.5 percent of GDP. Typhoon Haiyan to date will cost the Philippines 6.5 percent of its GDP. The people of the Philippines might live in shacks by American standards but far more of those shacks were destroyed.

The final death toll from Hurricane Katrina was 1833. A staggering number in a county as developed and organised as the United States. Sandy killed 73 people in the United States, and despite being reported as an American storm, it also killed 54 people in Haiti and 21 in seven other countries.

The final death toll from Typhoon Haiyan has yet to be established but it will likely exceed 6000. If that many people were ever killed by a single event in the United States it would remain the focus of media attention for years. But since it happened in the Philippines it is only worth a week.

Obviously each storm was a catastrophe to the people directly affected. Being the biggest or smallest, most expensive or least expensive is meaningless when your house is destroyed or loved ones are killed. But if the media paid attention to disasters outside of the United States there could be more attention and consequently more aid to the people who need it the most.

This is the kind of thing that bothers me after the fact. But we had more pressing matters to worry about in the middle of all the death and destruction.

Wednesday 20 November would prove to be a challenging day for my team. We were flying a 14000 square kilometre grid with more than a dozen pairings every day and at least four times as many legs. Our original objective of covering northern Cebu Island had expanded to the islands of Bantayan, Negros, and smaller islands in the vicinity. We were burning up about 900 pounds of fuel an hour. We had to refuel every time we went back to Bogo. Even if we did not need to I would have refueled every time anyway. There is no justifiable excuse for moving the aircraft one inch of an open flight plan without full tanks as long as the option to refuel is always there.

Our base of operations in Bogo was running short on fuel, medicine, food, water. Another shipment of supplies from Israel was due to arrive on Saturday but that was three days away. Between now and then we had to find and transport as many people as we could whilst exhausting as little fuel as possible. My support pilot joked that a brief jaunt to Hong Kong would have to wait.

We were transporting a patient from Bantayan Island to the field hospital in Bogo when one of the ground teams alerted us to a mother in distress. She was in labour and complications required immediate evacuation to the field hospital. She would lose the baby and possibly die herself without proper medical facilities.

We were still over Bantayan Island. Diverting to her location would take mere minutes. But we were already critically low on fuel. The weather was bad throughout the day and only getting worse.

There were downbursts between the two islands and the possibility of microbursts. The UH-60 is designed to function in extreme weather conditions but a microburst can take down a 747. If impacted by a microburst we would hit the ground like a watermelon thrown off the Eiffel Tower. This was an unacceptable option as far as I was concerned.

My original plan before we knew about the pregnant woman was to elevate over the cloud base. Going around it would exhaust too much fuel. Going over the primary storm foundation would leave very little margin for error. The only other option was to land on Bantayan Island and wait for the storm to proceed, which would take several hours. I was seriously considering the latter.

The flight surgeon wanted to pick up the pregnant woman and take her to the field hospital. People like her were the reason we were there in the first place. I decided to divert and remain at that location. The medical crew could treat the pregnant woman in the aircraft on the ground as we waited out the storm.

The Sikorsky UH-60 casualty extraction configuration has some impressive medical technology. It is a tiny hospital in the sky. I would rather be a medevac patient in this aircraft than a land patient in any of the damaged hospitals we saw in the Philippines. But it has its limits.

It can be an operating room if necessary but that mother and her baby would be better served by a full surgical team in the advanced facilities of the field hospital.

The medical crew wanted to take her to the field hospital. They could not save the baby otherwise. But diverting to her location made flying over the storm and all the way to the field hospital mathematically unlikely. At best, we would run out of fuel and have to land in Medellin where the baby and possibly the mother would die whilst waiting for ground transportation to the field hospital. At worst, we would run out of fuel over the Visayan Sea and kill everybody on board. My decision would have to be final.

The flight surgeon's primary responsibility is the medical care of any patients on board the aircraft. His job is to save lives. The pilot's primary responsibility is the safety of the aircraft and, by extension, everybody on board. My job is to fly and land in one piece. Those two jobs mostly correspond in harmony. Sometimes they contradict each other dramatically.

I had known and worked with the flight

surgeon on my team for two years. I knew full well that he believed with every fibre of his being that we should go to the field hospital. He also knew that once I decided not to go to the field hospital based on the safety of the aircraft and its crew there would be no way for him to change my mind.

He trusted that I knew how to do my job and he was professional enough not to let any hostility toward my decision show. He was a higher rank but he knew that ordering me to fly the aircraft his way would have been completely useless. No human being on this planet can give that order to the pilot in charge.

One of the first things they teach you when you train to fly medical evacuation is that the aircraft comes first. You might feel like putting the patient first but that would be a mistake that could cost people their lives. The loss of one person in the aircraft is dreadful but the loss of the aircraft itself generally means the loss of all lives on board. You cannot do this job without the ability to coldly calculate the greater good.

The pilot is there to fly from one point to another. Our decision making process and judgement are based on what is best for the aircraft. We cannot consider the needs of the patient. Most of the time that is in the best interest of any passengers on board. Sometimes it is not.

One of the second things they teach you in training is to pay attention to the weather. Adverse weather brings down more aircraft than anything other than human error. And flying in adverse weather is often the result of human error. The inexperienced pilot pushes ahead in bad weather. The more experienced pilot turns back to join the most experienced pilot who never took off in the first place. It is an old axiom that has proven itself time and again.

Medical evacuation regularly involves landing in alternate locations due to weather. Pilots have to be willing to land in some field that is not on the flight plan. Whether there are any patients in the aircraft or not is irrelevant.

These are some of the things I told myself while we were waiting for the weather to clear.

Spock once said that the needs of the many outweigh the needs of the few just before he pretended to sacrifice himself to save his ship. He was being melodramatic when you consider that he never intended to die. He was also a fictional character. But he was right.

We left Bantayan Island when it was safe to do so. The baby was already dead by then. By waiting for the storm to pass we had enough fuel to take a direct course and safely reach the field hospital. The mother died before we landed. The original patient that we were transporting before we diverted to the mother's location was treated at the field hospital and released a few days later.

Nobody ever said anything to me about it, and they never will, but I knew that my decision killed that mother and her child.

The field hospital treated 272 people on Wednesday, including 95 children. The day's reports included 4623 people confirmed dead, 18557 injured, and 1602 missing.

Military life is somewhat unusual to my way of thinking. Israel is a country where most people are in the military for at least a few years, sometimes less. Some people remain longer. Conscription of women as well as men takes away a great deal of the testosterone one finds in the militaries of most countries. Women in Israel can serve in any position open to men. There are more men in the IDF than women but there is no institutional gender discrimination.

The result is that women are free to do their jobs and do not have to waste time with misogyny and trying to act like a man to fit in. I am a woman who leads a team of men. Our genders are never an issue. I do not have to shave my head and spit on the floor to be respected. We do not regale each other with tales of our amorous adventures to prove how virile we are. We do it because we want to.

At the same time, I do not decorate the aircraft with flowers and posters of unicorns. There are a few reasons why that would be inappropriate. I have yet to wear a ballet tutu whilst on duty. I do not hide that I am female nor do I go out of my way to demonstrate the fact. I do my job. Just like every other woman in the IDF. Just like every man.

Part of that job requires the ability to display absolutely no emotion whatsoever in the face of abject carnage. I cannot appear frightened in a frightening situation. Any fear I show would only transfer onto the rest of my team. Imagine how you would feel if you saw the pilot on your flight trembling in fear. I cannot panic and run screaming through the aircraft. That would likely instill little confidence in the patients.

There is a famous incident of an American pilot who was forced to land a commercial airliner in the Hudson River when the engines failed. He became famous for remaining calm throughout the descent and water landing. I do not want to take anything away from his accomplishment but I think he would be the first to point out that remaining calm is an essential duty of any pilot in charge. It is necessary for the benefit of the people around the pilot and for the administration of the aircraft itself. Very few people make the right decisions whilst panicking.

When my decision to avoid the storm killed that mother and her baby I showed no emotion. I was as cold and calculating as a Vulcan. Sometimes you have to take a limb to save a life.

When I went back to my housing at the end of the day I cried like a little girl.

SIX

Thursday 21 November was the day of the animals for some reason. My team were preparing a patient for the flight from Bantayan Island to Bogo when a brown and white spaniel looking dog approached us. It might have been a kooikerhondje but I cannot say with any degree of certainty.

The dog was soaking wet as were we all. It started raining on Sunday night and was not about to stop any time soon. Wednesday had seen the heaviest storm since the typhoon itself. We assumed that the dog was hungry.

To this day I have no idea how many pets were killed by Typhoon Haiyan. We knew there were probably a lot of homeless pets looking for their owners but humans were our primary concern. Whatever spare food we had went to children and pregnant women first, then older people, everybody else. There was nothing left for the dogs. They were on their own.

One of our paramedics tried to scare the dog away but the flight surgeon found it more interesting and watched this dog intently. The flight surgeon is very much a dog person and has several large breed dogs at home.

I thought he was just being a dog lover and I gently reminded him that we were a little too busy to play with dogs at the moment. He decided that the dog had not come to us for food but was instead trying to get our attention. It had our attention but I was more interested in the task at hand.

For reasons I will never understand, the flight surgeon decided that the dog wanted us to follow it. I have no idea how he arrived at this conclusion. The dog was just looking at us and barking. There could have been a million different reasons. Or no reason at all. Dogs bark from time to time.

I wanted to leave and let the dog find somebody else to bark at. The flight surgeon wanted to follow the dog. He felt that it would lead us to one or more injured people. I felt that the rain was starting to take its toll. This man was a capable physician and excellent hallah baker but I doubted his ability to decipher the language of dogs.

The patient we were trying to get to the field hospital, or at least I was trying to get to the field hospital, was not seriously injured. He could wait but I felt that he should not have to. Especially if he was only waiting so that we could find out what some dog wanted. But patient care was not under my jurisdiction. The flight surgeon was in charge of medical decisions and he decided to listen to this dog.

The flight surgeon and one of the paramedics followed the dog, and the rest of us remained with the aircraft. I was actually hoping they came back with a boy who had been trapped in a well or some other proof of this dog's Lassie abilities. At least then it would not have been a waste of time.

Instead they came back with nothing. Not even the dog. It ran away as they were following it and they never found anybody in need of assistance. If the dog wanted them to follow it then it did a pretty lousy job of not running away too quickly.

A more likely explanation is that the dog noticed a giant machine with large twirling blades land in its backyard and it came over to us to investigate. We have all seen dogs chase cars but this might be the first dog I have ever seen try to chase a helicopter.

The patient was successfully treated at the field hospital. We never saw the dog again.

Several hours later the medical crew were stabilising a patient for transport when a bay stallion approached us.

We were all very surprised to see a horse. A dog is one thing. We saw dogs all over the place looking for food and families. The Philippines is like China when it comes to stray dogs wandering about. But a horse is a thing of a different colour. I was under the assumption that there were no horses in the Philippines. Probably because of Stanley Kubrick.

In the movie *Full Metal Jacket*, Debra Winger's husband complains about the lack of horses in Vietnam. Since many Vietnam War movies were filmed in the Philippines I may have made an unconscious association. Although *Full Metal Jacket* was filmed entirely in Britain. And there were no horses.

It turns out there are more than a few horses native to the Philippines as well as descendants from various Spanish and American colonisers. There is a tradition of horse fighting in the Philippines that likely involves gambling and alcohol. More so for the humans than the horses.

We saw no horse fighting whilst we were there. The people who enjoy that sort of thing were preoccupied with more productive endeavours at the time.

This particular horse approached us calmly. It showed no signs of fear or aggression so we assumed it was a domesticated horse. It probably wanted food but if we did not have enough to feed stray dogs then there was no way we would be able to feed a horse.

More importantly to our situation, we needed the horse to move a safe distance from the aircraft before we could take off. It was not afraid of us on the ground but our collective din was considerably quieter than a couple of 2000 horsepower turboshaft engines.

A rearing stallion could literally lose its

head under the titanium alloy rotor blades tearing through the air at 300 revolutions per minute. Even a smaller panicking horse could easily run into the tail rotor. That would not be so good for the horse. It would also leave us stranded on the ground until we could determine if the tail rotor was damaged.

One of the paramedics was volunteered to move the horse. How he was to accomplish this was anybody's guess. We were not a group of horse people. Our animal experience was restricted to dogs, cats, the occasional fish. But that horse had to go before we could. Somebody suggested firing a single round into the air. The sound might scare the horse away. It would also probably scare the patient and any other people in the vicinity who might hear it.

The paramedic tried chasing the horse but it was unimpressed. Apparently we were not threatening enough to scare away a fight or flight response prey animal. This instilled in us little confidence in our ability to defend our homeland. Fortunately, we are never the front line of defence. We are in the mezzanine.

The flight surgeon had a better idea. The oxygen distribution system within the medical interior of the aircraft has some kind of suction device that makes an ungodly noise. Anybody who is afraid of visiting the dentist would hate this device. The flight surgeon turned it on full throttle and pointed the suction hose at the horse.

I cannot say what kind of psychological

trepidation the average horse has with going to the dentist but the noise was loud enough or irritating enough to frighten this creature away. Or at least far enough away that we could finally take off.

It was only after this incident that we began to notice other horses. None came as close to us as this one had and most of what we saw was from the air. But we all agreed that we noticed far more horses after this one than we had before. It is just like shopping for a blender. If most of the appliance stores are out of stock when you are looking then everybody has hundreds of different models after you buy one.

Near the end of the day we found a cat. Or rather it found us. The paramedics were giving first aid to a little girl on the ground whilst the support pilot and I were reviewing our log books. The flight surgeon was trying to talk to the girl's parents in Spanish. I did not witness this exchange but I imagine it was amusing as neither the flight surgeon nor the parents spoke Spanish.

A small tabby approached the little girl. It was either an older kitten or unusually small adult. We all assumed it was hers until the parents displayed a surprisingly negative reaction toward the cat. It appeared as though they were afraid that this tiny ball of fur was going to attack their daughter. The cat, for its part, was about as threatening as a baby with a binky.

The parents made noises and gestures to

frighten the cat away. It was not particularly impressed but it casually moved away from the girl and closer to the aircraft.

We eventually determined through the use of body language and improvised hand signals that the girl was allergic to cat fur. The parents were not afraid of a kitten attack. They were afraid of an allergic reaction. Their hypersensitivity to this situation was justified by the fact that they were in an economic group that rarely has access to routine medical services. Simple allergies can be a serious issue when you have no medication. We were the closest thing to a hospital their daughter had seen since her birth.

We were ready to leave the area after we treated the daughter. There was no need to bring her to the field hospital. We gave them a limited supply of food and water. A ground crew would bring them more at a later time.

Before we could leave, the cat brushed up against one of the paramedic's legs. He picked it up and was immediately hypnotised by the cat's spell. He wanted to bring the cat with us but that seemed like an imprudent idea. Anybody who has seen a cat react negatively to being transported in a moving automobile can appreciate the risks of taking one on board a helicopter. It was not like we had a cat carrier packed away between the gauze and bag valve masks.

Most of us believed that feeding the cat and sending it on its way would be the best solution. Our food supply was all but gone at this point but feeding a cat requires considerably fewer resources than feeding a horse. The problem is that cats will not eat just anything you put in front of them. It is not like you can give a cat an MRE and be done with it.

The flight surgeon wanted to leave the cat to its own devices. He is a dog person, after all. I decided that as long as somebody could keep the cat under control then it could come with us. I am neither a cat nor dog person but I agreed with the rest of my team that this animal would likely die on its own.

Animal rescue was not part of our mission objective but there was no harm in bringing this cat to Bogo. Other than the possibility that it would become hysterical and scratch somebody. I felt that if that were to happen then our surgeon and paramedics could probably make use of the advanced equipment in the aircraft and treat a scratch.

The flight back to the field hospital was surprisingly calm. The cat was unperturbed by the motion or noise of the aircraft. It sat on its favourite paramedic's lap during most of the flight.

The cat was fed by somebody on the ground at some point in time. I was not involved as I had other priorities. I am not saying I had better things to do but I did. We all did. But people more emotional than I tend to be took a minute here and there to care for this new arrival. It was welcomed by much of the staff and became an unofficial mascot. I saw it from time to time wandering about the grounds, sleeping, eating, generally being the centre of attention.

Eventually it was adopted by a Filipino family. I think they named it Haiyan, which seemed strange to me. Partly because most of the people in the Philippines called the storm Yolanda and partly because naming your pet after the worst typhoon you have ever known strikes me as peculiar.

Outside of our animal adventures other IDF teams rebuilt two schools, and China sent the hospital ship, 和平方舟 (*Peace Ark*), with 100 medical personnel to the southern Visayas.

Friday 22 November was the day of anniversaries. It was two weeks after Typhoon Haiyan and the week after our first full day in the Philippines. Though weeks cannot technically be an anniversary. It was also the 50th anniversary of John F Kennedy's assassination. One was obviously more important to the people of the Philippines than the other two.

CNN on Friday devoted the entire day's international broadcast to the Kennedy assassination. This was an important historical event that permanently altered the United States and, to a lesser extent, other parts of the world. Its anniversary deserves to be mentioned on the news.

But my personal opinion is that news organisations, particularly television news, have a responsibility to inform the public of the day's events. Televised news perhaps has a greater burden than print news because people who rely on TV more than newspapers or other media tend to be less aware of whatever is going on in the world.

History is very important and historical events should be remembered. The 50th anniversary of an event is obviously going to generate more interest than the 49th anniversary. We humans prefer rounded denominations. But I think that telling people what is happening now is more important than reminding them of something they already know. Surely less than a full day's coverage would not have been disrespectful to the memory of a dead president or his country.

Conversely, ignoring the current pain and suffering of an entire nation is more than disrespectful to those people and their country. News by its very definition should focus more on current events than events that took place before most of the people reading the teleprompter were born.

The death toll in the Philippines had reached 5209 on Friday. 23404 people were injured and 1611 were still missing.

The Israeli field hospital in Bogo treated its two thousandth patient on Friday and rebuilt two more schools. The Canadians had treated over 400 people on Panay and were searching remote mountains on that island every day. They were clearing roads, building bridges, bringing supplies to the people on Panay and its outlying islands just as we were on Cebu and its islands.

The American, Japanese, Australian, and

other medical teams on Leyte treated over 9500 people. British and Chinese ships were rescuing survivors all over the western and southern islands of the Visayas.

Over 3000 foreigners were in the Philippines assisting with relief efforts. And CNN was talking about how similar the streets of Dallas look today as they did 50 years ago.

Such is the nature of information by television.

Friday was another rainy day and my team had a bit of a situation during transport of three patients from Bantayan Island to Bogo. None of their injuries were life threatening and they were all conscious during the flight. The rain was not especially heavy but there were thunderstorms and intermittent lightning strikes.

Flying a UH-60 during a lightning storm is not an occasion for alarm. The aircraft has a ballistically tolerant fuselage. It is designed to withstand direct impact from rocket propelled grenades and all manner of firearms. The outer hull is armoured as are the flight controls and even the flight crew's cockpit seats. The fuel tanks are crash resistant and encased in a self sealing material. The fuel cells will actually fix their own hole should anything ever puncture them.

The rotor blades include a titanium spar and fire resistant material that maintains operational integrity in the event that parts of the blades are destroyed. The tail rotor assembly includes a fin that acts as antitorque if the tail rotor is damaged.

The dangers of a lightning strike to a helicopter are damage to the flight controls, fuel tanks, and rotors. All of which are protected on the UH-60.

Commercial airliners are hit by lightning strikes all the time without any of the passengers on board even noticing. The fuselage conducts the electricity away from the interior. An aircraft in flight generates its own static charge. Though less powerful than a lightning strike it is also far more sustained than any infrequent lightning storm. If you could somehow touch the exterior of an aircraft in full flight you would be in greater danger than if you were in one that is struck by lightning.

Lightning can hit a person in their automobile without injury as long as they remain in the vehicle and do not complete the circuit. Lightning is simply not an issue in the context of our operations.

But the patients we were transporting during this particular lightning storm did not know any of this. One was in a state of panic and quickly causing the other two to worry more than necessary. The medical crew tried to calm them but people injured by a massive storm tend to be more sensitive to other storms. Particularly in a flying box that is not especially aerodynamic to begin with.

The medical crew were debating whether or not to sedate the patient when there was a quick burst of light outside the aircraft. I announced that the aircraft had just been hit by lightning and that all systems were fully functional. This was not entirely true as it was a burst of energy within the clouds and not technically a lightning strike. It never came close to actually touching the aircraft but my announcement made the patients feel a little better.

Much later, after the patients were in the hospital, the aircraft was secure, and everybody was warm and dry, the flight surgeon suggested that it might have been inappropriate for me to tell people that the aircraft had been hit by lightning when in fact it had not. Telling a patient that you have been hit during a lightning storm could very well have the opposite of the desired effect. The medical crew could easily have faced three panicked patients rather than just the one.

The flight surgeon was correct, of course. It is against protocol for the flight crew to address the patient during a medical procedure. I could say that I was concerned that the patient's state of mind posed a threat to the aircraft but that was never the case. The worst case scenario would have been for the medical crew to sedate the patient and calm would have been restored. Nothing that happened was beyond the medical crew's capabilities. My input was completely unnecessary.

This is likely the primary reason I have never flown passenger transport. I like to fly but I do not like answering questions or concerns from people who do not know anything about flying. Questions about air speed and ceiling ranges do not bother me so much as questions about safety and the acrobatic abilities of the aircraft.

Is it safe? Obviously. Millions of people use helicopter transport every day. If these helicopters were falling like rocks then they would probably be illegal in most countries.

What if the engine dies? A plane has wings to keep it in the air long enough to land but if a helicopter's rotor stops moving it will fall like a rock. I would rather be in a helicopter after an engine failure than in any fixed wing aircraft. Wings can help an aeroplane glide under the best circumstances but the aircraft can only land safely on limited surfaces.

Rotor blades on a helicopter do not stop if the engines fail. The ascendant flow of air keeps the rotor blades rotating as long as the aircraft is descending. Pilots are trained to perform a manoeuvre called autorotation in flight school and cannot get a private licence without demonstrating the ability to do so. The requirements for commercial certification are more strict than for a private licence and military requirements are greater than commercial requirements.

My first flight instructor always used to say that the moment you put yourself in a situation where an engine failure can kill you is the moment that it will. I can safely guarantee without hyperbole that any helicopter pilot in any advanced military has every ability to land the aircraft without a single engine.

What if the tail rotor fails? Will the helicopter spin wildly and crash like I saw in a movie? The tail rotor prevents the aircraft from spinning out of control as the main rotors generate considerable torque during normal flight. There is almost no torque during an autorotation and the aircraft can land safely without the tail rotor. People thought about and solved all of these issues a long time ago. There is likely no question you can ask that Igor Sikorsky has not already answered.

Can a helicopter fly upside down? Most cannot and there is no logical reason to do so even if it could. It might look cool to see a helicopter perform a loop but it serves no practical purpose.

I very briefly flew aerial photography over ten years ago in South Africa, mostly in the MD 500 and Bell 206. I enjoyed the 206 especially and the exceptional scenery but I did not care for the interaction between pilot and photographer.

They did not always understand that the aircraft was in my control and not theirs. They were more concerned with getting their shot than the safety of the aircraft and everybody on board. Had I done everything they wanted me to do I would have died several times a day. Some of these photographers were famous in their own little worlds and dealing with their massive egos was simply not for me.

Flying casualty extraction requires no

interaction between the flight crew and patient. In fact, it is best when only the medical crew address the patient's concerns and questions. Let them answer a million questions a day about how safe it is to fly in a helicopter. Meanwhile, I can look at the view outside my office window and whistle "Ride of the Valkyries" in my mind. Or out loud sometimes.

That almost has to be better than Tom Petty's "Free Falling".

SEVEN

Primary search and rescue operations were completed on Friday 22 November. We continued transporting a few patients from various evacuation centres to the field hospital but everybody who could be found had been found. There were still over a thousand people missing nationwide but most of them were likely lost at sea.

I spoke to an American about a month after Typhoon Haiyan hit the Philippines. He was confused as to why there were far more people missing after Haiyan than after Hurricane Sandy. I tried to explain that Sandy was a smaller storm and that it struck a much larger land mass. Haiyan hit a series of relatively small islands. North America is considerably larger than the Philippines. It was all of those islands spread out across the country that made getting aid to everybody a challenge.

My team specialise in casualty extraction but our focus on Saturday was medical transport and the new shipment from Israel.

The Israeli delegation came to the Philippines with 100 tonnes of humanitarian aid. But that was never going to be enough. By Saturday 23 November we were low on pretty much everything.

Our intention was always to leave behind enough medical equipment and supplies for the local medical personnel to treat any additional needs until the region's devastated healthcare infrastructure was operational again. But we used more medicine, food, water, fuel than anybody anticipated.

Another 100 tonnes of aid were transported on Saturday. It took most of the day to get the medical supplies from the airport in Cebu City to the field hospital 90 kilometres away. The main road to Bogo was open but there were still not enough ground vehicles to carry everything in a timely fashion. My team transported supplies directly from Cebu to save time.

We had not been to the airport on Mactan Island since we first arrived in the Philippines nine days earlier. I was surprised by how much had changed in such a short time. There was far less activity and far fewer people, though it was nothing close to a ghost town. The news reporters were long gone. The crowds cheering us when we arrived had since made their way to the field hospital. The constant flux of military aircraft taking off and landing had abated and the approach path was practically deserted. The airport went from the primary arrival point for most of the international delegations to the country's largest storage depot.

In addition to the supplies that had just come in from Israel there were palettes upon palettes of materiel from every corner of the world. The main helipad was full of supplies, forcing us to land on the light fixed wing apron. Much of the world donated and delivered supplies but most of the countries lacked the resources to transport those supplies once they were in the Philippines. It was up to the overwhelmed Philippine government to deliver aid from Cebu City to the rest of the country.

An endless queue of trucks was bringing medical supplies from the airport to the field hospital whilst my team transported mostly food and water to Bogo, Medellin, and Daanbantayan. We already knew which areas needed it the most. It was a simple task of going back and forth to deliver the aid to a lot of hungry and thirsty people.

The IDF had spent a great deal of time and money training us to extract wounded soldiers from precarious situations. That is our job and that is what we do best. Delivering bottles of water to people requires very little training or experience. But it was exceptionally rewarding.

We had spent more than a week telling the most desperate people that we had no food or water for them and we were only there for their wounded. It was heartbreaking to walk away from people whom we knew had not eaten in days. Ground teams were providing food the entire time but they were concentrating on the centralised evacuation centres and could not get to everybody. My team could reach more remote locations in less time than any ground transport. That was precisely why we were charged with evacuating the injured. But it was nice to bring something back rather than only take people away.

During one such trip to Bogo we found a man sitting at the edge of what used to be a sugar cane field and crying into his hands. He was not injured. His family was safe. His home was destroyed but that would be rebuilt in the coming weeks or months. He was crying because his crops were gone. When they went to the evacuation centre they had no idea how bad the damage would be. It was only when they returned to their home that they saw a year's worth of sugar cane completely destroyed. His income for the entire year was lost.

That is when I started to fully appreciate the financial impact of Typhoon Haiyan. We were concentrating on health and safety. A secondary concern was shelter. It never really entered my mind just how much this storm had affected their pocket books.

News reports will always tell you how much money a typhoon costs but that is incredibly relative. A hurricane in Florida that kills 10 people is going to cause more expensive property damage than a typhoon in the

Philippines that kills 1000 people. Nobody on Bantayan Island has a million dollar condominium next to a billion dollar shopping mall.

Typhoon Haiyan will never enter any record books as the most expensive typhoon but it ruined thousands of people financially. Millions were left homeless with few resources to rebuild. There is no way to know how many of those people will never recover. It will definitely never be mentioned on the local news.

All of the supplies and medical treatment we provided were free of charge. Obviously we were never going to send anybody a bill. I assumed that the Philippine government would help the people rebuild their homes with the billions of dollars they have collected from all over the world. Although that was a false assumption in the end. People actually had to pay their government for reconstruction or do it themselves with whatever materials they could find or buy.

What I had never thought about before talking to this man in the sugar cane field was that no organisation or agency could return lost wages from destroyed farms and businesses.

A shopkeeper in Bogo told us that she did nothing when people started to steal the food from her store during the looting before the IDF arrived and helped restore order. They were welcome to it as far as she was concerned.

Then they started stealing appliances. She understood the need for food but could not see why anybody needed a stolen microwave or washing machine. Her complete inventory was gone by the end of the day. She compared it to going into another person's bank account and taking all of their money. She did not know if she would ever be able to start her business up again. Her shop survived the typhoon but it could not survive the aftermath.

My team flew over countless farms. All of them were at least heavily damaged. Most of them were completely destroyed. What looked to me like bombed out fields were the only sources of income for almost a million people.

The economy was bad enough before Haiyan. The loss of almost 1 million hectares of agriculture, including much of the nation's fishing, sugar, coconut and egg production, about 300 000 tonnes of rice, and millions of small businesses will take years to replace. Areas of the country that were physically unaffected by the typhoon will feel the impact in their grocery stores as demand overwhelms supply.

Bogo before the typhoon was a thriving trade and commerce centre and one of the country's primary sources of agriculture. Almost all of that agriculture is gone.

The official death toll by Saturday was 5235. 24681 people were injured and 1673 were missing. Some of the survivors we encountered were completely defeated. They had lost loved ones, homes, pets, businesses, everything they had. All I could offer them were some boxes of food and bottles of water.

The amazing thing to me was how many of the people we encountered had positive attitudes. They had lost more than anybody ever should but they were determined to get on with it. We saw a lot of emotionally broken people and we provided the occasional shoulder to cry on but we saw even more smiling faces. They lost far too much but most of them were happy to be alive.

We were delivering food and medical supplies to Bantayan Island on Sunday when we heard that a helicopter had crashed. My heart immediately sank. I had no idea who went down, whether it was somebody I knew or a complete stranger. I did not even know if anybody survived the crash. But the last thing any pilot wants to hear is that another pilot did not make it. Most of us would feel bad if a North Korean pilot crashed. That country is batshit crazy but a pilot is a pilot.

Two Germans in a civilian helicopter were flying north from Aklan Province on Panay Island to Pampanga when engine failure forced them into Manila Bay. They had just delivered relief supplies to Caticlan and were returning to their base of operations.

A British transport crew located the aircraft off the coast of Bulacan near Manila but was not equipped for sea to air rescue and communicated the location to an American search and rescue team. The Americans extracted the pilots and handed them off to the Philippine Coast Guard. The pilots were in the water for only a few minutes and were uninjured. It was a truly international search and rescue operation.

One of the great things about helicopters is that they can land safely without any engines. But that generally only works on land. They do not land very well on water unless they are equipped with pontoons and even then land is always better than water. Most helicopters are not water tight and will sink fairly quickly, depending on size and weight. I have no information about the specific aircraft in this particular water landing but the pilots were in the water with lifejackets when they were rescued.

Sunday was a long and tiring day but we all felt good about the work we were doing. I went to sleep exhausted and looking forward to another exhausting day.

There were 5387 confirmed dead, 25074 people were injured, and 1708 missing.

Monday started as uneventfully as any other day. I woke up, fell out of bed, dragged a comb across the tangled beretta of what used to be my soft and silky hair. We had breakfast and our morning briefing. The day's mission was to bring supplies to Negros Island. Our search and rescue efforts were completely unnecessary when we went there the prior week. There were far fewer injuries than on other islands in the area. But they were as desperate for relief supplies as anybody else. The people on Negros Island were left just as homeless as the people on Panay Island.

We delivered supplies to the people on

Bantayan Island the day before and to Cebu Island the day before that. Today it was Negros Island's turn.

It was raining much like any other day but there was nothing especially noteworthy about it. There had been days with far heavier rain as there would be the following day. Monday was a fairly pleasant day by comparison.

A low pressure system developed over the northeast tip of Negros Island and western coast of Cebu Island directly in our flight path from Cadiz to Bogo. It was not especially worrisome but there was no reason not to divert to a northern course around Bantayan Island and approach Bogo between the smaller Batbatan Island to the northeast and Bantayan.

Over the Visayan Sea one of the paramedics reported smelling fumes in the cabin. We could smell nothing in the cockpit but it immediately got our attention. I went over a million different scenarios in about a second and thought that perhaps there was a pressure drop in the bleed air manifold and backflow through the heater but the heater was off. Maybe I was simply hoping this was the problem. It would have been easier to solve.

The medical crew then reported smoke in the cabin. This is never a good sign.

There are plenty of procedures in place in the event of smoke in the cabin. We went down the checklist and followed them by the numbers. The worst thing you can do in such a situation is to panic. Where there is smoke there is usually fire but sometimes it is a small and very manageable fire.

And sometimes taking the time to perform standard operating procedures gives the fire room to grow.

The smoke got thicker without giving us any indication of exactly where it was coming from. Putting out a fire requires knowing the location of the fire. I put the fire extinguisher switch to main but did not pull either T-handle since there was no warning light indication. The IR sensors were telling us nothing.

Pulling a T-handle sends a fire extinguishing agent into the engine compartment. Assuming the fire switch is on main or reserve. Pulling a T-handle also shuts off fuel to the associated engine.

The UH-60 can operate with only one engine but without any indication as to which engine to shut down it would be very easy to choose the wrong one. If you subsequently shut down the other engine you are left with nothing. Since we were over a fairly large body of water I wanted at least one engine in operation.

I knew that ditching was a very real possibility at this point but I wanted more information. The master alarm was silent. The fire alarm was obviously malfunctioning. I could try to land on Bantayan Island but that would expose everybody to increasingly heavier smoke and put them at greater risk should the situation escalate. There was only one option regarding the crew. They would have to go.

No pilot ever wants to leave their crew

behind, especially in the water. But everybody on board that aircraft was fully trained in water evacuation. The paramedics were used to jumping into water daily, albeit under different circumstances.

The locator beacon on the emergency life raft was operational before the medical crew were in the sea. The support pilot had sent out an emergency distress signal before he evacuated the aircraft and I communicated their location to our operations centre before diverting to Bantayan Island.

The British Navy light aircraft carrier HMS *Illustrious* had arrived in the Philippines that day. They were northeast of Panay Island and responded to our distress signal. They were farther away than Bantayan but a better option for several reasons. Given the choice I would prefer to be stranded on an aircraft carrier full of mechanics who could possibly assist the aircraft than on a small island full of storm victims struggling to survive. There would also be better tea choices on the British vessel.

But heading to the British ship exacerbated the probability of ditching in the sea. This was the day after two German civilians ditched in Manila Bay. I did not want to follow their example.

No pilot ever wants to ditch in the water but there was also an issue of pride. Military pilots tend to think of ourselves as being better trained and more experienced than civilian pilots. It is analogous to police SWAT officers and shopping mall security guards. There is a bit of an elitist attitude in some of our professions. I did not want to be the mall cop.

I also did not want to be the only pilot in the entire Philippines theatre of operations to lose a 30 million dollar aircraft. I probably thought about writing that incident report more than I should have under the circumstances. The only thing on my side was the fact that the international media had already abandoned the Philippines. If I lost the aircraft I would never hear the end of it at work but at least I would not have to hear about it on the news.

I had an independent oxygen supply so I could theoretically fly the aircraft all day without experiencing any adverse effects of smoke inhalation. But since I did not know what was causing the smoke I could not efficiently predict how far the aircraft was willing to go before a catastrophic failure. Bantayan Island was not my preferred location but it was the logical choice.

I was closest to the north end of the island where I knew there were more than enough empty fields. Haiyan had decimated most of the crops on the island, effectively making it one large landing zone. By the time I was over land the smoke in the cabin was thick and black so I came in heavy.

It was a deserted area and about as far away from the evacuation centre as you could get and still be on the island so I knew that I would not be putting any civilians on the ground in danger. The UH-60 can tolerate a vertical impact up to 38 feet per second. I came in just under that.

I have only landed harder on two occasions. One was intentional during a controlled training exercise and the other left me in a fair amount of pain for quite some time afterward. But the UH-60 is designed for hard landings. Even the crew seats are energy absorbent. It probably would have appeared more dramatic to those watching from the ground had there been anybody there but it was just another hard landing. I was more concerned with the billow of smoke emanating from the aircraft.

On the ground I activated the impact switch and the fire extinguishing agent was released in both engine compartments. The smoke stopped immediately and the air gradually cleared. I contacted my team who were safely floating in their raft. I then contacted our base in Bogo. Another search and rescue team had already been dispatched to my team.

The maintenance crew were transported to my location some time later and we went over every step of what occurred.

The aircraft was in no condition to fly back to Bogo so the maintenance crew remained on Bantayan Island whilst I went back to our operations centre. The rest of my team were already there and we discussed the possibility of being grounded for the duration of our mission in the Philippines. There was not exactly a surplus of helicopters lying around. If ours could not be repaired then we were done.

It was later determined that a control module failure prevented the IR sensor signals from reaching the warning panels. As one of my tactical flight instructors once told me, you can have the most technologically advanced equipment in the world but sometimes shit happens. There is an old saying amongst pilots that if something has not yet broken on your helicopter then it is about to. That law proved all too true on this day.

Had I pulled the T-handles it would have cut off fuel to the engines without releasing any fire agent into either engine compartment. I would have been left without engines but with more smoke, forcing me to ditch in the sea and park my helicopter at the bottom of the ocean. A minor emergency landing could have been much worse. As it was, the aircraft was reparable. There were no injuries and, even more fortunate, we were not transporting any patients at the time.

Monday's reports had 5469 confirmed dead, 25916 injured, and 1747 missing.

My team spent the rest of the day in Bogo, Medellin, and Daanbantayan whilst the maintenance crew worked on Bantayan Island. The flight surgeon and paramedics made themselves useful in the field hospital. The support pilot and I continued distributing supplies by land. The worst thing you can do to pilots is keep them on the ground but the people of Cebu Island still needed more of everything.

Handing out supplies by ground transportation was an unusual experience for me. We had spent the last ten days flying around the area, so I knew it well enough to recognise where we were at any given time.

But in an aircraft you have a certain distance between yourself and the people you are helping. Obviously in the air but also on the ground. You land, unload supplies or take in patients, take off. The aircraft acts as both a positive and negative magnet to the people on the ground. They quickly understood that a helicopter landing in their field meant rescue, medical treatment, food and water, whatever they were looking for in that moment. We were always swarmed by people any time we landed in a heavily populated area.

At the same time, people knew instinctively not to get too close. The sound of approaching rotor blades attracts those who need assistance but the sight of them scares the hell out of people.

On the ground there was no big noisy machine between us and the people. Nobody is afraid to come right up to a parked truck. We interacted with people every other day, certainly, but on this day we were like popes, with crowds of people wanting to touch us. Except that we were bringing physical rather than spiritual relief.

Speaking of popes, I think the current one should have visited the Philippines. It is an overwhelmingly Catholic country and such a visit would have benefited the people greatly.

There is nothing wrong with telling the world to pray for disaster victims but actually going to see them does far more for their spirits. Even Justin Bieber made an appearance a month after the storm. Surely the people of the Philippines can expect more from their pope than from Justin Bieber.

I felt like a general inspecting the troops when we drove into Medellin. We came with trucks full of supplies and I rode in the back of what Filipinos and Americans call a pickup truck. Mostly because I wanted to. Due to unforeseeable circumstances I became the ranking officer as soon as we went north of Bogo. I was not at all in charge of distribution and did nothing to interfere with the people who had been doing their jobs all this time. But I wanted to stand in the back of the lead truck and there was little anybody could do to stop me.

This was by no means an issue of ego. An actual general would have sat in the passenger seat. I simply wanted to see the landscape from a very different perspective from what we were used to and I rather like the movement and wind rushing by my face.

Pilots generally think of ourselves as superstars. As the old joke goes, how do you know when you are on a date with a pilot? After the first hour he says, "Enough about me. Let's talk about flying."

We were always greeted by cheering crowds when we landed in populated areas. But we spent most of our time taking away the injured. Most of the people on the ground wanted us to give rather than take. I quickly learnt that the teams on the ground were the real superstars. The people were far happier to see us arrive by land with trucks full of supplies than to land a helicopter with a few bottles of water. By air we were Ringo. By land we were Paul.

I also got a better workout on the ground, unloading trucks and passing out food and water. That was manual labour that did everybody good. When we landed the helicopter I often stayed in the aircraft. If we were there for longer periods we would power down and we all got out. But sometimes we were only on the ground for a limited time and the aircraft remained idle. Nobody has the time to power up a helicopter after every single landing. With a truck it is a simple matter of turning the ignition switch. Everybody got out and pitched in.

The absolute best part for me, from a purely selfish point of view, was that I got to see one of the schools. We heard about the infrastructure teams rebuilding schools but my team never got to see them. We heard about opening ceremonies with local politicians but we were never invited. We were always busy with other things.

On Monday there was another reopening ceremony with the mayor of Bogo and important community leaders. I have no idea if General Eizenberg was there. He attended some of the school openings but I cannot say if he was at all of them. Somebody from the senior staff must have been there.

I went to a different school on Monday; one that had been previously reopened. The school was full and classes were in session. There was no ceremony or fanfare so we did not get to see any song and dance routines. But we saw something much better. We saw children and their teachers in classrooms getting on with their lives. They were all very happy to see us.

I very briefly worked as a teacher several years ago. What I enjoyed the most about it was interacting with the students. But they were not always happy to see me. I was the one who gave them exams and assigned homework.

In Bogo all of the children were happy to see us. You can always tell when children are expressing honest emotion rather than simply saying what they have been told to say. These children were genuinely grateful.

We stayed long enough to feed the students lunch. It was nothing fancy but it must have seemed like a banquet to children who were already living in poverty before Typhoon Haiyan. One of the teachers told me that even the laziest students were happy to be back in school. She joked that they came for the food we provided since it was better than their usual lunches. But I am sure they were just as eager as everybody else to return to the stable environment of the school after such an enormous storm.

A little girl of about six or seven years

called Maganda approached me and looked like she had something to say. I crouched down to her and she looked right into my soul and said "shalom". The word meant nothing to her. Somebody told her to say it to the Israeli strangers. But I could see in her eyes that she could not have been more sincere.

I wanted to adopt her and take her home right then and there. But I doubt her parents would have appreciated that. I had to struggle to stop thinking about the children like her who did not survive.

No matter what we did or failed to do in the Philippines or what was to come, no matter who would complain about our motives or how much people who know nothing about us will never stop hating us, the heartfelt gratitude from that little girl gave all of our efforts purpose. She was not a Filipino thanking an Israeli, a student thanking a soldier, a Catholic thanking a Jew. She was a person thanking another person from one heart to another.

EIGHT

For several days I helped one of the head nurses at the field hospital translate her reports into English. This was nowhere near the scope of my job responsibilities but we were all there to help the locals as well as each other. She was a PhD candidate at the time and decided to utilise her experience in the Philippines toward her doctorate. This made perfect sense since her dissertation was on disaster response and recovery as it pertains to nursing.

What frustrated me about trying to help with her reports was not all the medical terminology and dry academic writing style, which presented its own challenges, but that she used Google to translate from Hebrew to English. I then tried to translate the Google English into actual English.

Google is sufficient for translating single words but it is illiterate when it comes to sentence structure, grammar, idioms. Google gave us sentences like "Correlation nursing informed consent experience patient autonomy attitudes in four domains product moment correlation coefficient." I had to translate random words into English sentences.

Had she simply wanted to translate her Hebrew into English then she could have used somebody with a better grasp of Hebrew. More than a few of the delegation knew English better than I know Hebrew. But as one of the few people on site originally from an English speaking country I was her first choice to turn her Google gibberish into genuine English. I have a good deal of experience with gibberish and I am often loquacious in English. Weather permitting.

She wanted to credit me as a translator on her paper but I told her it was completely unnecessary. I was not especially confident in the work I did for her. Translating medical reports from one language to another is an art form. Translating from Google to an actual language is like throwing darts after a few too many pints.

Tuesday 26 November was our last full day in the Philippines. Things were looking a lot better for the people whose lives were disrupted by Typhoon Haiyan but there was still a lot to do. There were still 1726 people missing. 5560 were confirmed dead and 26194 were injured.

Our helicopter was repaired and ready to get back to work. We had plenty of supplies to deliver and my team were anxious to get on with it. The weather, however, was unwilling to cooperate.

It rained on and off the entire time we were in the Philippines. Mostly on. We saw blue skies here and there. Mostly it was grey. Sometimes it was black. As a parting gift perhaps, Tuesday was one of the darker days.

We were transported to Bantayan Island where we swapped places with the ground crew. They went back on the aircraft that brought us there and we went back on the aircraft they worked through the night to repair. Most of the ground crew went to sleep as soon as they reached Bogo. The maintenance chief stayed awake just in case there were any issues with the aircraft that would require his attention.

Both the maintenance chief and I signed off on the airworthiness of the aircraft. We had every confidence on paper that everything was fully functional. But I was still going to take every precaution.

We were scheduled to pick up supplies from the airport in Cebu and spend the day in Daanbantayan and Medellin. We were on Bantayan Island. The only way to fly from one island to the other is to go over water. Such is the nature of islands.

This is not ordinarily an issue but the more you think about your aircraft bursting into flames the less you want to fly over water. You never want to catch on fire over terrain either but at least you can land the aircraft at a moment's notice.

A typical flight from Bantayan Island to Cebu City would take you over the Tañon Strait and southeast over Cebu Island. Given our situation I decide to take the scenic route. We flew to the eastern centre of Bantayan Island and hopscotched over the smaller islands that lead to Cebu Island. This took longer but it also meant that we were never over water for more than nine kilometres at a time.

Once we reached Cebu Island we simply followed it south to the airport on Mactan. This route also took us over Bogo where we could have landed at the field hospital if necessary.

As it was, the maintenance crew did an excellent job and there were no further issues with the aircraft. We picked up our supplies at Mactan-Cebu Airport and headed north to Medellin. From Medellin we went north to Daanbantayan. After that we were back in Bogo.

There was far less excitement on this day. But excitement is the last thing you want during relief operations. There is nothing routine about disaster recovery. The goal is to return life to the routine.

Our last full day in the Philippines was relatively uneventful. We did not save any lives but we did not lose any either. We delivered food, water, medicine, and shelter supplies to the people of Daanbantayan, Medellin, and Bogo. Before we knew it our day was over. It seemed to all pass by in a blink.

I can remember the first time I went to Disneyland. Despite seeming like an abrupt tangent it is relevant to the subject at hand. I spent several days before going to Disneyland in anticipation. I was not entirely a child but everybody is a child to some extent the first time they visit Disneyland. I waited anxiously for that day to come. And then it came. And went. Before I knew it the big event I had been looking forward to was over and done with.

I spent the better part of eight days studying the Philippines and planning and preparing my team's mission. Diving into a disaster recovery operation is not quite the same as going to Disneyland but there is still a level of anticipation before the fact. You do not exactly look forward to witnessing so much pain and suffering but you are eager to get to work.

Before we went to the Philippines I was unsure if I was fully prepared. I knew that my team could perform the task ahead of us but I was not certain that I had adequately researched the area and the needs of the survivors. Many of my concerns quickly dissipated as the day's events unfolded. It takes surprisingly little time to consider yourself an expert during extreme situations. Before I knew it our mission was over and it was time to go home. Much like my first trip to Disneyland, I was only getting started.

I woke up very early Wednesday morning. I did not really sleep all that much Tuesday night. We had a busy day ahead of us and yet we were doing nothing for the people of the Philippines. But it still takes some effort to move an army of volunteers to the other side of a very large continent.

It rained most of Tuesday night but stopped rather suddenly at about 0300 Wednesday morning. I went outside to watch the clouds drift away. It was the middle of the night but still quite warm. It was still typhoon season, after all. It never got cold regardless of how much it rained. It was always a warm rain. And it was humid every second we were in the Philippines.

Once the clouds cleared, the stars put on a spectacular show. That was something I do not generally get to see. Israel is basically one giant light bulb at night. It takes some effort to get away from city lights to a point where you can truly look at the stars beyond a few flickering lights here and there.

The Philippines is generally dark outside of Manila. The lack of steady electricity after the typhoon made it even easier to see the heavens. There were no electric lights as far as the eye could see outside of our base of operations.

I grew up in a time and place where watching the stars at night was both entertaining and possible. We had no Twitter when I was a child. But we had the cosmos.

I still get a sense of satisfaction in seeing that there is infinitely more to our universe than the petty problems we make for ourselves on our little planet. Looking up at the stars that night made me feel better about everything I had experienced in the preceding days. The number of stars in the sky was far greater than the number of people who died in the Philippines. It was even greater than the number of people on Earth who exhibit utter indifference toward all those deaths in an island nation far removed from their way of life.

People were already packing equipment before I started wandering about the compound. By the time the sun rose pretty much everybody was awake and active.

Our intention was always to leave behind some equipment and as many supplies as we could. Most of the larger medical equipment was given to the Severo Verallo Memorial District Hospital. Some of it was given to the German and Austrian delegations which were scheduled to take over the Cebu area after we left. Generators, tents, medicine were given to the evacuation centres in and around Bogo. Additional medicine was given to the Cebu government to distribute as needed.

Somebody somewhere probably knows the monetary value of all of the equipment and supplies but none of that matters to me. When you give a starving man a loaf of bread he never asks how much it is worth. Nor should you congratulate yourself for giving him the five euro bread instead of the one euro bread.

Every member of the Israeli delegation volunteered to go to the Philippines. Some of us were technically on the clock, as it were, but most of the teams were reserve officers. They had regular jobs outside of their work with the IDF. That is probably something that most people do not realise. Most of the national delegations sent military teams to the Philippines. They were all doing their day jobs, as were my team. Most of the Israeli delegation were volunteers who were not being paid to go to the Philippines. We all left our families and homes but they left their jobs as well. It was an easy decision to make.

Family is the most important thing in Israeli life, in Judaism, and I would hope in every other country and culture in the world. The importance of family makes it easier to leave them behind in order to help other families in another part of the world. We missed our families whilst we were away but knew that Filipino families were suffering. There is no point in having strength and ability if you do not use it to help others.

The Israeli field hospital treated 2686 patients, including 848 children, and delivered 66 happy babies. Treatments ranged from emergency surgery to simple first aid and everything in between, including psychological counseling.

Some of the treatment had nothing to do with Typhoon Haiyan. People were given artificial limbs, cancer treatment, eye exams. Some people got glasses, hearing aids, canes for the first time in their lives. Two children were brought back to Israel with our delegation and their parents for cleft palate surgery that required a more advanced hospital setting.

Six schools were repaired by IDF infrastructure teams. Two were reopened just after the typhoon and the other four were reopened after they were rebuilt. Psychologists treated students and teachers for disaster trauma recovery. Teachers were taught how to engage students in structured recovery programmes. Teachers and school officials throughout the Visayas attended IDF seminars on student counseling in the aftermath of the typhoon.

We were there to bring humanitarian aid, treat the injured, help with search and rescue efforts, feed people, and rebuild houses and schools. Our mission was never to transform the Philippines into what we thought it should be. We were there to help the country get back on its feet. We achieved our primary objective once all of the area hospitals were fully functional. This was what the Philippine government asked of us.

By Tuesday we had delivered relief supplies to the islands of Cebu, Negros, Bantayan, and more than a few smaller islands in between. We treated thousands of people at the field hospital, at evacuation centres, in small cities, in the middle of nowhere. We found everybody that could be found and transported a few thousand people to evacuation centres and the field hospital.

We gave food and water to more people than I could ever count. We did what we could to help the people of the Philippines when they needed it the most. There will be reports and lists of which countries supplied how much money and who did what. Some countries did more than Israel. Some did less. All that really matters is that people who had the means helped people in need.

Israel has a long history of sending humanitarian assistance anywhere in the world when it is needed. Saving a single life to save the entire world is a core concept in Judaism. It makes no difference whether the people in those countries are Jewish, Christian, Muslim, Hindu, Buddhist, atheist, rich, poor, pink, brown, yellow, orange or blue.

The IDF has sent noncombatant humanitarian personnel to some of the least likely places, including Cambodia, Lebanon, Armenia, Cyprus, Romania, Croatia, Palestine, Rwanda, Kenya, Turkey, Greece, Kosovo, Macedonia, Sri Lanka, Egypt, Japan, the United States, Bulgaria, Ghana, and now the Philippines.

IDF relief personnel will go to countries that Israel does not officially recognise and countries that want Israel wiped off the map. Humanitarian missions are neither political nor military. They are not to help the governments but to help the people. Many of whom have no say in how their political leaders make decisions.

Many other countries do the same. American personnel will go almost anywhere in the world after a natural disaster. Everybody knows about the United States. They are large enough and influential enough to have a media presence wherever they go.

Most of the people on this planet have no idea how much countries like Israel, Japan, France, Kuwait, China do for others. China did as much as any other country for the Philippines. Their efforts were likely all over Chinese media but how often were they mentioned on BBC.

I am a native of South Africa and will always take a certain level of gratification in that country's accomplishments. Most of which are just as unknown to the world at large as all of the good that Israel does. But when it comes to humanitarian aid, my adopted homeland makes me far more proud than my native land ever could. Just as the international media mostly ignored the effects and aftermath of Typhoon Haiyan, they also prefer to ignore everything that Israel, and a great many other countries, do for people in need. Humans are an exceptionally charitable species. Even, believe it or not, in countries where English is not the primary language. The people of Asia, Africa, South America are just as capable of showing compassion for their fellow man.

Over 11 million people in the Philippines were affected by Typhoon Haiyan. To date, 6033 people are confirmed dead, 27468 injured, and 1779 are missing. The typhoon caused over PHP 35 billion in damages, almost half of which was agricultural. Rebuilding infrastructure is a painfully slow process but fast and easy compared to regrowing crops.

Most of these numbers will likely rise in the coming weeks and months.

Typhoon Haiyan hit Micronesia first but it was not yet a category 5 super typhoon. The Philippines was the first to feel the full impact of the storm so that is where it caused the most damage. But when it was done with the Philippines it also hit China and Vietnam.

I never saw any international media coverage of any countries outside of the Philippines but the typhoon destroyed 9400 homes and affected over 3 million people in China alone. Those are not insignificant numbers. Yet China still sent a substantial delegation to the Philippines.

Typhoon Haiyan also killed at least 18 people in Vietnam and 8 in Taiwan.

The people of Cebu were treated to a concert by local musicians on the Saturday after we left. The concert was held in the Don Celestino Martinez Coliseum where we originally set our base of operations.

No international celebrities have yet announced a benefit concert for the people of the Philippines. Maybe this will change some day and I will be proved wrong. I hope so. If a storm in London or New York caused even half this level of destruction everybody you have ever heard of would play at the concert.

Musicians and artists like to consider themselves compassionate humanitarians so I am sure they are capable of showing as much compassion for a small country in Asia as they are for large European and American cities where they can charge more for concert tickets. A few of them recorded a song or two for Africa in the mid 1980s. That was pretty recent as far as caring about Africa goes but maybe now it can be Asia's turn. Unless George's and Paul's concerts in the 1970s filled the quota.

The Israeli delegation officially left the Philippines on Wednesday 27 November. After two weeks of rough camping we were all loaded back onto our comparatively luxurious El Al 747s for the 15 hour flight back to Tel Aviv. The conversation on the flight to the Philippines was mostly about how we would best achieve our mission objectives. The conversation on the flight home was mostly about how inconceivably horrible the situation on the ground really was.

We were as prepared as any group could be when we arrived but statistics, reconnaissance charts, intelligence reports never tell you the human story. Reading about how many people were dead and how many more were expected to die is nothing like walking through a field of corpses rotting in the oppressive humidity and stagnant bacterial flood waters. It is easy to ignore that every number on a piece of paper is a person who left behind grieving family and friends. It is exceptionally difficult to ignore the human equation whilst seeing, smelling, feeling so much human carnage.

There was a big ceremony when we arrived in Tel Aviv with Benjamin Netanyahu, Moshe Ya'alon, and Benny Gantz all giving speeches.

I personally found it all rather unpleasant,

not only because these are not the best public speakers in the world, but also because I feel that we should help others because it is the right thing to do. We should not do it to congratulate ourselves. I would prefer if the international media recognised that countries outside of Western Europe and one or two in North America exist but I do not want us to blow our own trumpets all day just because CNN cannot find us on a map and BBC wants us off of it. The only speech that was not self serving was by Philippines ambassador Generoso Calonge. He seemed genuinely grateful for our assistance to his country.

Adding to the festive atmosphere was the fact that we arrived home on the first day of Hanukkah. It is a relatively minor festival and has nothing to do with going to or returning from the Philippines but I suppose any excuse to light a candle is good enough. We love our candles.

When I got to my house I just sat in a chair and thought about everything that happened. I assume I will be thinking about it for a long time. I did not host a party and announce to the world that I am the greatest humanitarian ever known. I cannot celebrate whatever I may have done whilst thinking about all of the people who have suffered and who continue to suffer. Writing this book is one way to process all of the information, I suppose.

I was just getting used to the Philippines when it was already time to leave. We saw horrible devastation everywhere we looked but we also saw beautiful tropical island scenes and crystal blue waters. The air was mostly very clean. I cannot say if that is typical or the result of an enormous typhoon followed by weeks of rain. But for a city dweller such as myself it was nice to be out in the fresh air every day.

Walking around the compound on that last morning I knew that what I will remember the most about this experience will be the people. They lived through the worst that nature can engineer but we saw more smiles than tears. We met people struggling to survive in hopeless situations but they all had hope.

I cannot say I am glad that any of this happened but I am glad that I went there to do what little I could. My efforts were a drop in the ocean but Maganda's smile made it all worthwhile.

EPILOGUE

The dust has settled and the TV cameras are long gone but recovery operations in the Philippines will continue for years to come. People are still hungry and homeless, and need all manner of supplies to rebuild their lives and care for themselves and their families. Several reputable relief organisations are assisting the people of the Philippines. All are very grateful for any donations they receive.

Some people say that donating to charities is a bad idea. They say that too much money goes to administrative and operating costs and not to the people who need it the most. We all want to give food to families in need, not pay some charity's fuel bills. But paying the fuel bill makes it possible for the charity to deliver food to the families in need.

Many of the islands of the Philippines are difficult to reach. Most are only accessible by boat or aircraft; machines that do not operate on good wishes. People cannot be fed unless somebody pays for the vehicles that get the food where it needs to go.

Money is always the best donation. Relief organisations working in the area know where and how to best utilise their resources.

Food is a great thing. Everybody likes food. But donations of food are often inappropriate for the location. What you would want to eat in a disaster situation might not be what people on the other side of the world eat. Food also has a habit of going bad. Sending rotten food to starving people is never ideal. Aside from the food itself, how it is delivered is a consideration. Canned food does little good for people who have no can openers. That people who have lost everything they own would happen to have a pocket knife handy is a specious assumption. Money sent to relief organisations can buy more appropriate food.

The Philippines currently needs medicine. But donations of open containers of ointments and expired prescription medications are completely useless. People always donate their used medicines after a disaster. Their motives are sincere but no relief organisation is going to deliver unsanitary materials that may be hazardous to the recipients. Donations of money can be used to purchase appropriate medications.

Donations of clothing can also be highly ineffectual. A well meaning American clothing manufacturer donated crates full of heavy coats and winter clothes to Indonesia after the December 2004 earthquake and tsunami. Indonesia sits on the Equator and has a humid tropical climate. They dress in winter the way most of us dress in summer. Money would have been more useful as a means to purchase environmentally appropriate clothing.

The people of the Philippines are rebuilding millions of homes. Building materials are absolutely essential. Yet donating materials can be problematic. The Philippines is a very humid country. The type of wood used in their houses might not be the same wood used in your location. Some countries do not even use wood in their homes at all. The way in which the buildings are constructed might be very different from construction methods in your country. Donations of money can be used to purchase building materials locally that are far more appropriate for the climate.

What about water? Everybody on the planet needs water to live. It should make no difference whether the water was bottled locally or in Colorado. Surely a donation of thousands of bottles of water would be welcomed.

Actually, not so much. The organisation to which you donate all that water must come to you to retrieve it. Then they have to transport it to the nearest airport, transfer it to an international airport, transfer it again to local airports in the Philippines, transport it from the local airport to a distribution centre, load it onto ground transportation, and drive it into affected areas for distribution.

At this point the relief organisation has now spent far more money shipping your water than it would have cost to simply buy the same amount of water from local businesses. An equivalent donation of money could be used to create and install a water filtration system that would service the community for years to come.

But beggars can't be choosers. People in need should take what they can get. This idea is flawed for several reasons. The people of the Philippines, or any area affected by a massive natural disaster, are not beggars. They are the victims of a natural disaster. Such events take place all over the world, regardless of income or productivity.

The people of the Philippines should be treated with as much respect as the people of New York or Tokyo in similar situations. If you would not want to receive torn and stained SpongeBob underwear then you should not send such a thing to others. Imagine how you would feel after a natural disaster if a relief worker gave you a discarded Kazakh horse bridle generously donated by a family in Mongolia. Donations are supposed to help people. They are not a garbage dump.

There are currently warehouses full of donated items in the Philippines that simply cannot be used. Personnel who could be delivering useful relief supplies are instead unloading and containing these items that will never do anybody any good.

Donations in kind use up valuable resources. Items that can never be used only take up space that could otherwise hold more beneficial materials. Useless items take up manpower that could otherwise be used to help people.

They also help to damage the local economy. Money can be used to purchase useful items locally, improving the economic situation for local businesses and providing needed aid at the same time.

Donations in kind are best saved for when relief organisations ask for specific items. The Philippines is not a backwards village in some distant jungle somewhere. It is an industrialised country with highly developed disaster recovery procedures. The national and local governments were largely unprepared for the massive destruction of Typhoon Haiyan but they are experienced with typhoons and other natural disasters. Philippine recovery agencies and relief organisations have a better understanding of what is needed locally than the rest of us.

It is true that some charities are largely self serving but doing a little research and finding out how the charity operates and where its funds go is an easy way to separate the many good organisations from the few bad apples. You can always look around and see which groups have done what work if you are unsure. The Philippines needs donations right now but they will also need donations next week, next month, next year. This is not a situation in which being first is best. Charitable donations are a good thing at the beginning of a disaster when it is all in the news. But donations are just as welcome further down the road after the disaster and the people affected by it have long been forgotten.

Some of the proceeds from sales of this book, minus publishing costs and taxes, will be donated to the International Committee of the Red Cross.

A few relief organisations with transparent operating procedures assisting the Philippines:

Habitat for Humanity
http://www.habitat.org/asiapacific
E-mail: ap_info@habitat.org

International Committee of the Red Cross
http://www.icrc.org/eng/
E-mail: man_manille@icrc.org

IsraAID
http://israaid.co.il/
E-mail: israaid@gmail.com

Médecins Sans Frontières
http://www.msf.org/
E-mail: office@msf.org.hk

Oxfam
http://www.oxfam.org/en
E-mail: information@oxfaminternational.org

Philippines Department of Social Welfare and Development
http://www.dswd.gov.ph/
E-mail: mail@dswd.gov.ph

Philippine Red Cross
http://www.redcross.org.ph/
E-mail: prc@redcross.org.ph

UNICEF
http://www.unicef.org/
E-mail: manila@unicef.org

ABOUT THE AUTHOR

Meira bat Erachaim was born and raised in South Africa, went to university in the United States, and lived and worked in China before settling in Israel.

She has worked as a helicopter pilot, documentary filmmaker, English teacher, and is currently a casualty extraction and medical evacuation combat support officer with the Israeli Air Force. In her spare time she climbs mountains, swims naked, and irritates her mother.

Her first published book, *Letters To Friends*, received high praise from the five people who read it. Her second book, *Fortnight in the Philippines*, details search and rescue operations in the aftermath of Typhoon Haiyan.

The controversial *Venom of Asps* was followed by *Her Whole Darkness in Motion*.